An Introduction to Supply Chain Management

An Introduction to Supply Chain Management

A Global Supply Chain Support Perspective

Edmund Prater

and

Kim Whitehead

An Introduction to Supply Chain Management: A Global Supply Chain Support Perspective

First published in 2013 by
Business Expert Press, LLC
222 East 46th Street, New York, NY 10017
www.businessexpertpress.com

ISBN-13: 978-1-60649-375-5 (paperback)

ISBN-13: 978-1-60649-376-2 (e-book)

DOI 10.4128/9781606493762

Business Expert Press Supply and Operations Management collection

Collection ISSN: 2156-8189 (print)
Collection ISSN: 2156-8200 (electronic)

Cover design by Jonathan Pennell
Interior design by Exeter Premedia Services Private Ltd., Chennai, India

First edition: 2013

10 9 8 7 6 5 4 3 2 1

Printed in the United States of America.

Abstract

In order to succeed today you must speak different languages. This doesn't necessarily mean Chinese, German or English. Rather it refers to the need to speak, accounting, finance, marketing and operations. This book is written for the executive who is not a supply chain management professional but who wants to learn more about his or her supply chain. We will do this by diving into some best practices, examples of how other companies have managed their supply chain, and getting an overall briefing on the state of the art in supply chain management today. Questions and topics will be brought up that will help you have an informed discussion with the supply chain management professionals in your company. As prior supply chain and manufacturing executives and now educators, we hope to share with you a mix of our professional and academic experience and knowledge that will provide you a framework for understanding the placement of your supply chain within the global marketplace.

Keywords

supply chain management, value chain perspective, global marketplace, forecasting, logistics, distribution, inventory management, supply chain uncertainty, chaos management, supply chain coping strategies, information technology and the supply chain, customer service and the supply chain, service operations

Contents

SECTION 1

Getting Started

Introduction

Dollar General opens two new stores every day. Where the company 10 years ago took weeks to launch a new store, it now has the process down to eight days, or fewer. The secret isn't Miracle-Gro. Instead, there's a well-honed choreography of human muscle and precision logistics that sets up each new outlet in little more than a week. Within the allotted eight days, the store management team moves from the setup of the first IBM point-of-sale terminal to the opening of the store. This is possible only if you have a strong logistics and supply chain management methodology and well-managed execution.

When the property managers at headquarters get the word that construction is finishing, a corporate buyer orders two to five point-of-sale terminals online, which they get by day 2 of an eight-day store opening cycle. The cash register order kicks off an electronic alert to the company that provides the satellite hookup between those registers and Dollar General Headquarters. The company that provides the satellite hookup receives an e-mail with the phone number of the new store. Knowing when the registers are due, the company then schedules an installer to arrive at the new store on day 4 or day 5, replete with gear to make the links.

When the physical setup of a store starts, a "setter" keeps the process moving as the onsite project manager. A setter's formal title is store merchandiser. His task is to deliver a just-in-time store, steering a crew of about 20 unpackers, stockers, sweepers, and fix-it people. Setters, also called "openers," erect shelves, install the point-of-sale registers, oversee the creation of the satellite uplinks, put up signs, and put out merchandise. They coordinate deliveries from suppliers and technology vendors, test accounting software, handle inquiries from headquarters, and sweep the floors when they're dirty.

All of this is done within eight days. To you, as the consumer, it all happens seemingly overnight, and suddenly a Dollar General store appears in your area.

The coordination and integration that it takes to execute a process like that shown above for Dollar General is something that world-class companies do every day. That is not to say that the execution is perfect in every instance, but it is to emphasize that managing a supply chain can appear seamless to your customers if it is managed aggressively, as part of the overall business strategy, and with continual changes to meet the needs of the customers.

This book is written for the executive who wants to learn more about managing his or her supply chain by diving into some best practices, examples of how other companies have managed their supply chain, and getting an overall briefing on the state-of-the-art in supply chain management today. As prior supply chain and manufacturing executives and now educators, we hope to share with you a mix of our professional and academic experience and knowledge that will provide you a framework for understanding the placement of your supply chain within the global marketplace.

We begin by introducing the concept of supply chain management. This concept has been steadily evolving for the last 30 years. From originally being seen as solely the tactical elements of distribution and logistics, the meaning of supply chain has grown to be an inclusive, overarching, competitive business strategy. Their meaning is embedded within an emerging network view of organizations that focuses on competition at the network level. In this view, organizations are competing supply chain to supply chain (network-to-network) within a global economy, a stark contrast to the old paradigm of organization-to-organization competition within a local economy.

After introducing the most recent paradigm of the global supply chain we continue the introduction by discussing strategy and globalization. This section discusses globalization, relationship management, and customer service. We suggest that strategy should drive the tactical components of the supply chain. Strategy must determine the "how to" in supply chain management or you are in danger of putting the cart before the horse. We have seen it happen and the results are dismal. We will guide you toward putting strategy first.

The second section of this book is entitled SCM Components. This section springboards forward from strategy and discusses the various tactical components of the supply chain and how they work together. The discussion is not intended to be all-inclusive, rather, we discuss elements that are central to supporting the strategy and provide an executive perspective of each. These elements include forecasting, inventory management, distribution, uncertainty, and information technology.

The final section of this book offers a view of the future. We encourage you to always challenge the way that things are done today and to be ever vigilant in looking for changes in your environment that may require your supply chain to adapt accordingly. As companies begin to compete network-to-network, it becomes ever more important to understand your supply chain, its flexibility, reliability, and role within your competitive global strategy.

This book is organized around the following diagram representing a global supply chain. We will refer back to this diagram from time to time to emphasize the network and systems nature of the supply chain and to make sure that we are providing a clear representation of the supply chain.

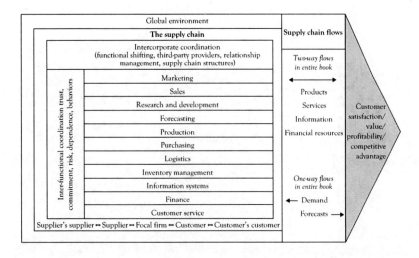

In order to help you navigate the book, each chapter includes:

Chapter Objectives providing focus

Key Take-Aways for yourself and your team

Reflection Points for you to consider and apply to your company and its current and future supply chain activities

Additional Resources so you may explore topics further.

We want to encourage you to

Make notes on the pages as you read, go ahead and dog-ear the pages—it won't hurt the book, and it will help you.

Not feel as though you have to read the chapters in order—go to whatever interests you most. This book is written so that it can be used more as a reference book than a narrative.

CHAPTER 1

Getting on the Same Page

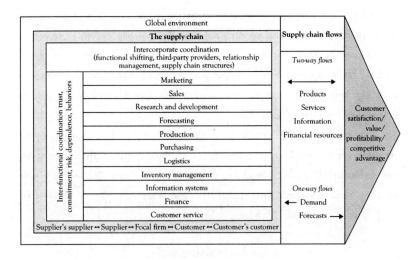

Chapter Objectives

- Define terminology
- Introduce the concept of "supply chain management"
- Explore the pillars that support excellent supply chain management
- Lay the foundation for the introduction of supply chain strategy

The Supply Chain

Supply Chain Management (SCM) is an umbrella term that incorporates many different ideas and concepts. In order to make sure that we are all "speaking the same language," we must first define the key terms we will be using throughout our discussion. Why is this important? A common understanding of words is important to any type of communication.

Simply stated,

> *The difference between the almost right word & the right word is really a large matter—it's the difference between the lightning bug and the lightning.*[1]

In our case, this is of practical importance. For example, some of the SCM articles, books, and so on you might see or discuss will use terms such as *supply chain* and *logistics* interchangeably, while these two terms actually refer to very different concepts. To avoid that type of misunderstanding, this section provides you with a reference list of key definitions that we will use in our discussions.

It is important to ensure that you and your teams (internal and external) are always on the "same page" when it comes to definitions; or, well-intentioned projects will fail simply due to misunderstanding one another. Time spent assuring coordination is time well spent and is one of the pillars of successful SCM.

Definitions

The Supply Chain

> *The supply chain comprises the sequence of companies that contribute to the creation and delivery of a good or service to end customers. This goes from the point of origin of raw materials and subcomponents all the way to the point of consumption.*

Internal—The **internal supply chain** consists of different departments, ranging from procurement to customer service. The supply chain includes activities associated with inventory (materials) acquisition, storing, production, transit, packaging, and delivery to customers. The activities are planned, executed, and monitored under the guidelines set by the company's chosen customer service levels and in line with the company's other operating goals.

Integrated—Once a company expands its viewpoint outside its corporate structure to look at suppliers and customers, it is concerned with an **integrated supply chain** that incorporates these other players.

Reverse—Depending on the industry, product, or both, there exists a **reverse supply chain**. The reverse supply chain includes the companies and processes that are necessary to return all or part of a product from the consumer to the point of origin. The reverse supply chain facilitates reuse, remanufacturing, recycling, and responsible disposal.

Supply Chain Orientation

Supply Chain Orientation is a systems perspective of the tactical components within a supply chain. This is a general business philosophy or way of doing business.[2]

Supply Chain Management

Supply chain management is the cost effective organization of the flow and storage of materials, in-process inventory, finished goods, and related information from point of origin to point of consumption to satisfy customer requirements.

Goal of Supply Chain Management

The goal of supply chain management is to evolve a company's supply chain into an optimally efficient, customer-satisfying process, where the effectiveness of the whole supply chain is more important than the effectiveness of each individual department or group.

1. Supply Chain Management focuses on business *processes* and their integration:
   - product design
   - planning/forecasting
   - order management
   - inventory management
   - order fulfillment
   - return management

Instead of *functions:*

- sales
- purchasing
- production

The primary method of doing this is by developing *relationships* among the individual supply chain participants.

2. SCM activities include:
- Forecasting demand
- Selecting suppliers
- Ordering material
- Receiving and managing inventory
- Shipping and delivery
- Organizing information exchange

Logistics

Logistics is the management of the storage and flow of goods, services, and information within a company or supply chain in order to meet customer requirements.

1. Elements of *Logistics* include*:*

Materials Management:	Sourcing and receiving of raw materials or unfinished products for subsequent use.
Material Flow System:	The ability to locate and schedule material through to end production and disposition.
Physical Distribution:	The delivery of finished goods to customers.

2. Logistic steps include:
- Forecasting demand
- Supplier ordering
- Scheduling production
- Accepting a customer order
- Receive and enter or accept and validate Electronic Data Interchange (EDI)

- Credit clearance/authorize
- Delivery commitment
- Inventory management
- Delivery to customer
- Return approval and acceptance

The order of these steps may vary based on product type, customer requirements, industry, or at the discretion of management.

History of Supply Chain Management

The term *supply chain management* was first used by two consultants by the names of Oliver and Webber in 1982. However, this term did not just magically come into being. Instead, Oliver and Webber had a good view of the future because they were standing on the shoulders of the Japanese and the Just-In-Time revolution of the 1970s. In order to get a better understanding of what constitutes a supply chain, consider the role of traditional performance indicators (cost, speed, flexibility, dependability, and quality) and how they function within business processes. Each is singularly important, but yet, each is dependent on one another within an interdependent system.

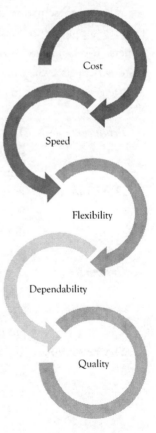

Given this reality how should we respond and manage them?

The Japanese responded with a process known as Just-In-Time (JIT) inventory controls. JIT combines the traditional performance indicators into a single outcome goal. The goal of JIT is to have a product at the right time, at the right quantity, and with perfect quality. Likewise, the goal of SCM is to have the right product, at the right time, at the right place, at a competitive price.

Three supply chain strategies facilitate the movement away from the traditional measures for supply chain management to JIT: flow orientation, plant orientation, and production orientation. Continuing this idea, in migrating from JIT to SCM, the following views must change:

- from flow-oriented to interfaces-oriented;
- from plant-oriented to relationship-oriented;
- from production-oriented to customer service-oriented.

But How Do You Make This Change?

SCM is concerned with the relationship between a company and its upstream and downstream partners; building relationships helps companies coordinate (work jointly) with their trading partners in order to integrate activities along the supply chain to meet customer requirements.

Who are these partners? As can be seen in Phase 1 of the following figure, a supply chain consists of a company and its suppliers and customers. This can be extended. Your immediate customer may have other customers of its own, while your supplier may have other subsuppliers. This general structure can be extended to include five categories.

Producer: This is the company that either manufactures some product (such as a lawnmower) or provides some service (such as a lawn-mowing company).

Distributor: Purchases bulk quantities of manufactured goods from the producer and sells to other companies in large quantities—much larger than individuals would purchase, also known as a wholesaler.

Customer: A customer may be an individual who buys a product for personal use or an organization that buys products to be resold or used to build other products of their own manufacture.

Service Provider: There is a host of providers of services in areas such as logistics, finance, human resource management, information technology systems and support, marketing, design, and the list goes on.

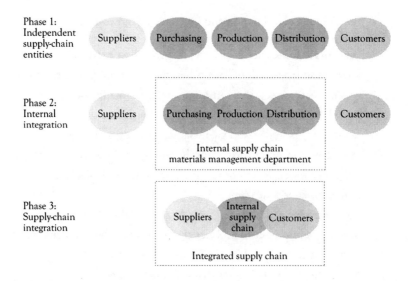

In Phase 2, a firm begins to realize that instead of treating each part of the supply chain as a separate entity, it should begin to integrate functions. This allows a firm to look for solutions that are best for the company as a whole, not just what's best for each individual department or business process.

In Phase 3, a firm expands its viewpoint to incorporate all upstream and downstream partners. This integrated supply chain is the long-term goal of SCM; however, you are limited by your supply chain's ability to *coordinate* activities and *integrate* different departments and companies. These two issues have different demands and structures. Specifically,

- **Integration:** How closely supply chain entities operate as a single unit—focus on interfaces (structure). This is a static process.
- **Coordination:** How seamlessly information, material, and finances flow within the supply chain—focus on movement (process). This is a dynamic process.

The interaction of these two concepts supports the structure of the supply chain and facilitates SCM.

Without strong coordination and integration your company may have

- **Inaccurate forecasts:** When each organization produces forecasts independent of each other, the uncertainty in the system is increased. This can result in the bullwhip effect. The bullwhip effect refers to the inventory phenomenon where small changes in demand create larger and larger changes in inventory balance further up the supply chain where the inventory resides. Graphically, the phenomenon looks like a bullwhip, hence the name.
- **Low capacity utilization:** If you forecast a large demand and purchase equipment to produce that quantity, what happens if the demand isn't as large as forecasted? You have a lot of money tied up in machines that aren't being used.
- **Excess inventory:** If you have produced a large amount of product in anticipation of high sales and those forecasted sales do not materialize, you have a lot of money tied up in these "extra" products and the cost to store them.
- **Obsolete inventory:** If you have large amounts of excess inventory, these items tend to become obsolete over a period of time. This means that the inventory can become outdated, no longer desired by your customer, or both.
- **Inadequate customer service:** If your forecast is too low, then you won't have products available when customers want to purchase them. This can result in lost sales and decreased market share.

All of these problems, stemming from weak coordination and low integration, can cause substantial difficulties for your company, in both reputation and financial stability.

Focusing on *integration*, there are several key issues that must be addressed in order to make all the individual groups and companies in a supply chain operate in unison. They include:

- **Choice of partners:** costs, organizational culture, potential, specialized know-how, taxes, exchange rates, and so forth.

- **Interorganizational networking:** independent versus dependent; secretive versus sharing; long term versus short term; win-win strategy versus maximizing own profits, and so forth.
- **Leadership:** At least some decisions should be made for the supply chain as a whole. Aligning strategies along the supply chain requires some form of leadership.

Likewise, *coordination* also has three key issues to consider. These issues allow groups in the supply chain to share information about current operations and future decisions.

- **Utilization of Information Technology:** Capture and use of historical data, demand forecasting, sharing information instantaneously, and EDI, B2B, B2C, and so forth.
- **Process orientation:** Use of performance indicators to determine weaknesses, bottlenecks, and waste within a supply chain (productivity, cycle time, safety stock, work-in-process, return-on-investment, etc.) are examples of process orientations.
- **Advanced planning:** Advanced planning incorporates long-term, mid-term, and short-term planning levels.

In essence, *coordination* and *integration* provide the framework for you to build your company's supply chain "house" (see subsequent diagram). As shown, in order to support your SCM "house" you and your team should have relevant knowledge in

- Logistics and transportation
- Marketing
- Operations management and research
- Organizational behavior, industrial organization, and transaction cost economics
- Cost accounting
- Purchasing and material management

When you incorporate these topics, you have the following housing framework:

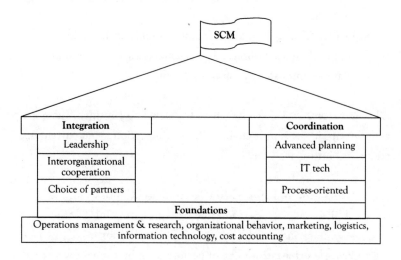

Another way of looking at this is to view it as a Value Chain issue. Michael Porter, in his classic book *Competitive Advantage*,[3] developed the concept of the Value Chain in which a company is divided between primary and secondary, or support, activities. Primary value chain activities are those that are directly involved with producing a product for sale and delivering it to the customer. They culminate in the total value delivered by an organization. The "margin" depicted in the diagram below is the same as added value. (All of the following is adapted from *Competitive Advantage*.)

The value chain

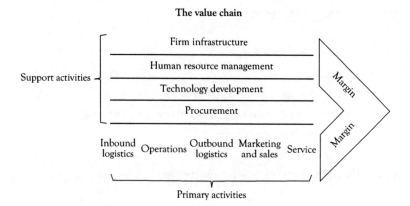

Thus, we see that viewing the supply chain as a value chain activity provides us with basically the same viewpoint as the "house" of SCM. Whichever viewpoint you take, your chain is only as strong as its weakest link. Or, if you prefer the house analogy, if your foundations are weak, the house will fall. The major focus of SCM is on primary value chain activities. Secondary activities such as information technology, while extremely important, are support activities.

Key Take-Aways

- Managers often overlook ensuring that everyone on their team is using the same terminology. **Keep everyone on the same page**, discuss the meanings of ideas, how concepts are interpreted in your organization, and so on. Remember that new employees may bring different definitions and concepts to the table based on their prior experience. You'll be amazed at the differences you find between even your longest tenured team members as to their understanding of concepts such as the supply chain.
- Remember that your supply chain partners come from different corporate cultures and perhaps even different national cultures. **Don't assume that your communication is clear or that you are using terminology in the same manner as your trading partners**. This is true in every aspect of negotiations or business processes. Show your partners how much you are invested in the process by ensuring that understandings including terminology are clear. This is important in an informal, as well as formal sense. In our international experience, informally ensuring that everyone understands concepts in the same way is extremely appreciated by international partners, because they see it as an attempt to truly work together, and not as adversaries.
- Listening is a key element that drives communication and ultimately leads to coordination and integration. As noted by Feargal Quinn, Superquinn's CEO and Ireland's Pope of

Customer Service,

*"Genuine listening ability is one of the few true forms
of competitive advantage."*[4]

- SCM calls for changes:
  - From flow-oriented to interfaces-oriented
  - From plant-oriented to relationship-oriented
  - From production-oriented to customer service-oriented
- SCM's excellence depends upon relationships.
- Integration and coordination are the pillars of successful SCM.
- The focus of SCM is on the primary activities of the firm.

Reflection Points

1. How does your team ensure that communications are clear and they are using shared meanings? Is it possible that communication problems are at the root of many intra or interdepartmental frustrations, complexities, or conflict? When is the last time you and your team discussed the "art" of communication including listening?

2. Does your company go the extra mile to ensure that concepts are understood the same within your company as well as with your trading partners? Have you experienced any situations of potential miscommunication, scratched your head, and were satisfied to call it a "minor misunderstanding"? Are misunderstandings in a supply chain ever minor?

3. How can you and your team work toward ensuring that meanings are shared throughout the supply chain?

4. How well do you and your team listen to each other and to your trading partners? This doesn't mean just reading and responding to e-mails. It includes trying to understand the perspective of the other party, looking for potential misunderstandings, proactively working toward shared meanings, and opening channels of communication.

5. When was the last time you asked yourself about the relationships your company has with its upstream and downstream trading partners? If this is only done informally, how will you know if everyone

on your team agrees to the type of relationship in place with your partners so that the relationship is managed in a coordinated fashion?

- Are they friendly?
- Hostile?
- Long-term?
- Short-term?
- Competitive?
- Win-Win?

6. Does your firm have an integrated view of supply chain management, or does each department fend for itself? Why or why not?

7. What is the history of your company? How do you think its history has impacted the way its supply chain system has evolved?

Additional Resources

Cottrill, K. (1997). Reforging the supply chain. *Journal of Business Strategy 18*(6), 35–39.

Davis, T. (1993, Summer). Effective supply chain management. *Sloan Management Review* 35–46.

Fawcett, S. F., Magnan, G. M. (2002). The rhetoric and reality of supply chain integration. *International Journal of Physical Distribution and Logistics Management 32*(5), 339–361.

Fisher, M. L. (1997). What is the right supply chain for your product? *Harvard Business Review 75*(2), 105–117.

Mintzberg, H. (1994). Rethinking strategic planning part I: Pitfalls and fallacies. *Long Range Planning 27*(3), 12–21.

Stock, G. N., Greis, N. P., Kasarda, J. D. (2000). Enterprise logistics and supply chain structure: The role of fit. *Journal of Operations Management 18*, 531–547.

CHAPTER 2

The Global Stage

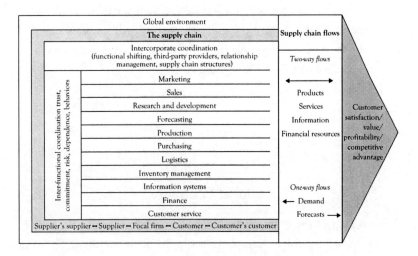

Chapter Objectives

- Introduce the types of global supply chains
- Explore the forces that affect the global economy
- Discuss the consequences of globalization
- Examine entry strategies for foreign markets
- Consider supply chain strategies

Global Supply Chains

Different types of firms exist and compete in the global marketplace. We distinguish them, at a high level, in the following ways.

The Multinational Firm

- Majority ownership in foreign sales organizations, distribution networks, or production plants
- Active in more than one country

- May have a borderless global culture, tailor production, and marketing to local needs such as Proctor & Gamble and McDonalds

The Global Firm

- Coordinated production, sales, distribution, and administrative networks that focus on singular products that do not have to be adapted to a large degree for individual markets. Examples include Coke, Walt Disney, and Sony.

The Domestic Firm

- All others

Global Economy

Within each of these types of firms, it is no surprise to practitioners of SCM that global forces impact daily supply chain decisions. To better understand this impact, companies in general, and supply chain managers in particular, need to ask three questions that will drive the rest of our discussion:

1. What are the forces shaping the global economy?
2. What are the consequences of globalization?
3. How can we take advantage of the dynamic globalization process?

What Are the Forces That Shape the Global Economy?

Market Forces

Market forces tend to be the issues that are immediately seen from a competitive perspective. For example, when there is increased competition, it is more difficult to compete in the local foreign market. A classic example is the growth of foreign competition in the automotive market. In the 1960s, the US foreign market generally consisted of the "Big Firms": AMC, Mercedes, BMW, Porsche, and Jaguar. Contrast that to the worldwide auto market of today. The increase in global market competition has led to shorter product lives, more customization, and faster response to market demands. For example, automobile manufacturers now come out with a new model in less than 4 years; earlier, they worked in 10-year cycles. There are key implications to this change:

- The traditional life cycle approach to international production is no longer valid.
- Simultaneous product development is needed in all markets (domestic and foreign).
- Local presence and representation is needed to facilitate customization and fast response.

The US international product life cycle approach first took the view that companies would introduce a product in their home market. After the new introduction phase, the product would move into high volume production and as the product matured and costs were minimized, production would be moved offshore and begin to be sold to overseas markets. This model no longer holds. Today, simultaneous product development and release is necessary in all worldwide markets. In addition, a local presence is needed in all worldwide markets to allow firms to customize their products to meet local requirements and respond quickly to any market changes.

Technological Forces

A presence in state-of-the-art markets is useful to a company for maintaining its technological edge. Examples of state-of-the-art markets include:

Japan:	semiconductor process equipment, consumer electronics, machine tools
Germany:	machine tools
Korea:	cellular phones, wireless products and services
United States:	aerospace, computers, software

These markets tend to have groups of companies with the same specialty working in close proximity to one another. This location strategy allows multiple companies to draw from specialized employee pools, be close to raw materials, increase access to knowledge bases (such as universities), and allow for co-location of suppliers. Production facilities in these markets also serve as market sensors, which allow supply chains to have advanced notice of changes in the marketplace. The consequential formal and informal networks of people, knowledge, and other resources facilitate growth and learning at both organizational and industrial levels. They also serve as learning laboratories to try out new technologies and services.

Global Cost Forces

Increased global competition has reduced costs. To use the automotive market as an example again, there has been a 30-year decrease in costs on automotive technology, parts, and vehicles. This has been driven by the fact that many growing countries help subsidize the growth of heavy industrial production firms, such as those in the automotive industry, in an effort to expand local jobs. This has led to a worldwide glut of production capacity driving down costs.

Labor costs are also being reduced as many US firms are moving jobs overseas where labor costs are lower. Overall, however, within the worldwide business community, there has been a shift away from off-shore strategies that are driven solely by a low-labor cost mentality. This is because of the diminishing importance of direct labor cost in the production of many products. Accordingly, there has been a reduction in what we call "island hopping" syndrome—where firms have moved from producing in Japan to Singapore, to Hong Kong, to Malaysia, to China, and so forth in search of the lowest labor costs. Instead, new competitive priorities are driving global location. These include priorities such as

- access to markets;
- access to skilled workers;
- quality;
- availability of suppliers;
- reliability of suppliers;

- transport time and costs;
- financially secure suppliers;
- socially responsible suppliers.

Political and Macroeconomic Forces

Because of the increase in free trade and the reduction of tariff barriers, international competition continues to increase. Likewise, there has been an increase in global trade groups to support organizations that are trading globally. These include, but are not limited to

- Asia-Pacific Economic Cooperation—**APEC** (Pacific countries);
- European Union—**EU** (Europe);
- Mercado Comun del Sur—**MERCOSUR** (South America);
- North America Free Trade Agreement—**NAFTA** (North America);
- South East Treaty Association—**SEATO** (Australia, New Zealand, Japan, Hong Kong, South Korea, Chile).

In addition, the development of regional free trade groups forces companies to rethink regional production strategies; examples include the EU and NAFTA. While these trade organizations and General Agreement on Tariffs and Trade (GATT) have been successful in reducing official trade barriers, countries still impose nontariff barriers, which favor the globalization of production strategies and their attendant supply chains. These nontariff barriers include, but are not limited to

- voluntary export restraints (United States, Japan: autos);
- trigger price mechanisms (US semiconductor and steel industry);
- local content requirement (European auto and semiconductor industry);
- technical standards and health regulations;
- government procurement policies.

What Are the Consequences of Globalization?

In general, the consequences of globalization on supply chains can be grouped into three areas:

- Increasing cooperation among logistics and operations areas of different members of the supply chain
- Functional integration, both internally and with joint ventures
- Search for improved geographical integration including knowledge, technology, raw materials, and so forth.

Increasing Cooperation Among Logistics and Operations Areas

One international indication of this trend is the growth of global third party logistics providers. These firms help integrate logistics, operations, and other supply chain functions. This is done not just by providing basic logistics functions, but by also offering logistics information systems and Enterprise Resource Planning (ERP) capabilities to integrate in other supply chain functions of the firm they are providing services to.

Integration of Internal Functions, Both Internally and with Joint Ventures

Within the automotive market there are joint ventures between GM-Toyota, Chrysler-Mitsubishi, and Ford-Mazda to name a few. All these are focused at streamlining technology and product development and reducing costs. Another reason for global integration is the increasing capital intensity of production facilities. For example, semiconductor plants' capital requirements have been

- 1986: $50m–$100m
- 1994: $250m–$400m (R&D over $1b)
- 2004: $1B
- 2010: $1.8B

By pursuing these integrated joint ventures, manufacturers share costs and risks. Several firms such as Texas Instruments and Hitachi, Motorola and Toshiba, and IBM and Siemens shared production facilities for DRAM chips.

Entering Global Markets

A firm has several entry options for entering into new global markets. Each of these options has implications for each type of trading such as purchasing, production, sales, and so forth. Our intention is to introduce you to the options that are available from a supply chain perspective; however, they apply to other processes and strategies within an organization as well.

The available entry options include:

- **Exporting**—Tapping foreign markets through marketing channels;
- **Licensing** (also **Franchising**)—Operations granted to the licensee in exchange for lump sum payment, per unit royalty fee, or proportion of profits;
- **Joint Venture** (also **Management Contract**)—Ownership split agreement;
- **Wholly Owned Subsidiary**—Locating own operations in a foreign site.

These options are also known as *strategic alliances* when the firm chooses to enter into a cooperative agreement with one or more firms to facilitate their entry into a new market. The exchange can involve financial remuneration, goods/services, information, or a combination of the three. The nature of the strategic alliance usually depends on what complimentary resource the foreign company is looking for in its local partner. When the firm chooses an entry option that does not include a foreign partner it is considered a *stand-alone entry*.

Key Take-Aways

- Every organization is affected by globalization in one way or another. Managers should be aware of the factors that drive globalization effects such as
  - Global market forces;
  - Technological forces;
  - Global cost forces;
  - Political and macroeconomic forces.

  These forces should be addressed proactively and a part of every overarching business strategy.
- Entering global markets can be done through the use of strategic alliances or stand-alone entry. The options available to facilitate entry into new markets and break down barriers include exporting, licensing (franchising), joint venture (management contract), and wholly owned subsidiary.

Reflection Points

1. What have been the impacts of the global marketplace on your company?
2. What are the current global market forces that your firm has identified that affect your business and industry? How can you be certain that all market forces have been identified, categorized, and addressed that are important to your company?
3. What impacts does your company make on the global economy?
4. What barriers to entry have kept you out of new markets? What options are available to you through strategic alliances to break down those barriers?

Additional Resources

Bovet, D. (2004, January/February). Europe's new growth driver: The supply chain can open the door to higher profits and more streamlined operations for companies operating in Europe. *Supply Chain Management Review* 9–17.

Omar, A., Davis-Sramek, B., Myers, M., & Mentzer, J. (2012). A global analysis of orientation, coordination and flexibility in supply chains. *Journal of Business Logistics 33*(2), 128–144.

Yip, G. S. (1982, September). Gateways to entry. *Harvard Business Review* 85–91.

CHAPTER 3

Supply Chain Strategy

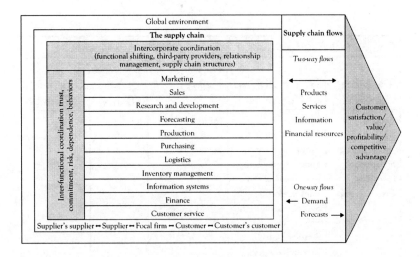

Chapter Objectives

- Continue discussion of strategic trading relationships
- Consider supply chain strategies
- Introduce types of supply chains
- Acknowledge uncertainty and variability

Supply chain strategy should first be based upon the firm's competitive position within the global market. No matter the domesticity of the firm, it is affected in some way by global competition or trading partners. As mentioned in Chapter 2, strategic alliances are necessary for global operations. They come in many different forms and types depending on the needs of your company. Keep in mind that as the needs of your company change, these alliances will necessarily need to change as well. Accordingly, you do not want to create stumbling blocks for yourself along the way by entering into strategic alliances that are not flexible enough to support the dynamic nature of your company, whatever that may be.

Strategic alliances are not only crucial for global operations; they can provide key competitive advantages. We have both experienced the advantages of having a strong relationship with a key vendor. In our experience, intercompany relationships are critical to any type of product or service you plan to produce or provide to your customers.

Contractual Agreements		Equity Agreements		
Traditional Contracts	Non-traditional Contracts	No New Entity	Creation of New Entity	Dissolution of Entity
Arms-length Buy/sell contracts Franchising Licensing Cross-licensing	Joint R&D Joint product development Long term sourcing Joint manufacturing Joint marketing Shared distribution Shared service Standard setting Research consortia	Minority equity investments Equity swaps	Joint ventures	Mergers Acquisitions

Established relationships should be "cherished"—yes, we know that word is not "business-like," but it should be. By cherishing relationships you build trust and commitment in ways that cannot be done by following a checklist in a book. Cherishing is a behavior that is not taught in business school. This behavior includes giving care or shelter to something, treating something as though it were valuable, sustaining and nourishing something with care, especially in order to promote, increase or strengthen it, nurse, nourish, sustain.[1] Ultimately, this is what makes strong, long-lived companies their ability to cherish relationships with their trading partners, customers, consumers, and other stakeholders.

SCM focuses on relationships. In this chapter, we provide you with an introduction to some of the key relationships for managing and sustaining your supply chain. These relationships can be categorized by level of commitment and strategic importance as shown in the following figure.

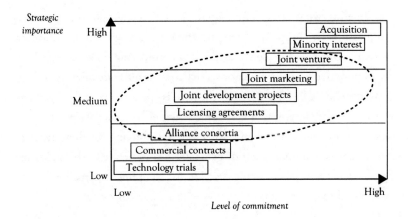

Level of commitment

Partnerships and Purchasing

Strategic alliances tend to be assessed and approached from a high level, strategic perspective of a firm. On a more operational, day-to-day level, partnerships with suppliers are the most common and are usually managed through the purchasing department.

The key thing to remember is that instead of choosing suppliers purely based on low cost (which tends to mean that you have a large number of suppliers you can chose from), you chose a few suppliers that you can build a long-term relationship with. Thus, the criterion for strategically entering relationships with suppliers differs from the traditional approach of simply choosing suppliers.

Traditional Approach	Supplier Partnerships
Primary emphasis on price	Multiple criteria
Short-term contracts	Long-term contracts
Evaluation by bids	Intensive and extensive evaluation
Many suppliers	Fewer selected suppliers
Sharing based on relative power	Equitable sharing
Improvement at discrete time intervals	Continuous improvement
Problems are supplier's responsibility	Problems are jointly solved
Clear delineation of business responsibility	Quasi-vertical integration
Information is proprietary	Information is shared

Outsourcing

Firms cannot be good at everything and sometimes turn to outsourcing noncore activities. The decision to make (inhouse) or buy (outsource) is a key managerial decision for both products and services.

Deciding what should or should not be strategically outsourced is unique to each company. There are some general guidelines, however, that we recommend be considered when considering outsourcing. First, the importance of the product or service to your ultimate offering to your customer should be considered. If the item is critical to your final product you need to maintain as much control as possible over its production, quality, availability, and so on. Therefore, outsourcing for these types of critical core components is not generally recommended. The following figure refers to the outsourcing decision for component parts, but can be generalized to other items or services within your company.

	Low → Criticality of the part to final assembly → High	
High Strategic value of the part in isolation **Low**	**Novelty** (outsource/in-house) Technology quality	**Proprietary** (in-house) Technology quality service
	Commodity (outsource) Price	**Utility** (outsource) Co-operation service

Criticality of the part to final assembly

In practice, three of the four quadrants in the figure above tend to be fairly easy to decide; however, the upper left hand quadrant, Novelty items, is the most difficult. It is this type of product that requires a "gut check" decision to be made because outsourcing this type of item creates the greatest risk.

If a decision is made to outsource, the question then becomes "Who will you outsource this product or service to?" Remembering that a key issue in SCM is relationships. The following criteria should be considered in outsourcing and partnering decisions.

1. Is there already a mature and trusting relationship with the best supplier in the category that could be further leveraged?
2. Does the prospective supplier have strong engineering capabilities?
3. Would this relationship create a lot of transactions that would create the need for an on-site representative from your organization?

4. Is the technology in the category changing at a revolutionary pace?

5. Does the category involve proprietary or core technologies?

Functional and Operational Strategy

Once a firm has a firm grasp of its global position, it may begin to strategize how it will compete. Next, the firm must consider with whom they will create trading relationships. When those decisions are in place, the firm can look internally toward how it will execute its competitive strategy. We will focus on how a company chooses to compete and how that drives functional and operational strategy decisions within the varied internal functions of the firm. Ultimately, there are only two competitive strategies:

- Cost
- Differentiation

The Differentiation strategy can be broken into subgroups such as

- Quality
  - High performance design
  - Consistent quality
- Time
  - Fast delivery
  - On-time delivery
  - Product development speed
- Flexibility
  - Customization of products
  - Volume production flexibility

The key thing to notice is how a company's choice of competitive strategy drives other decisions. If you decide to compete on cost, then your supply chain must be geared to drive down costs at each opportunity. This is the competitive position of Wal-Mart. Wal-Mart chooses suppliers that can provide low-cost mass produced products and utilizes low-cost sea, truck, and rail logistics.

On the other hand, if you decide to compete by differentiation, there are other decisions to make. Will you be competing on speed? Design quality? Conformance quality? Brand image? Each of these differentiation strategies (and there are more) requires a different type of supply chain. To visualize this, compare the supply chain structure of Wal-Mart (competitive strategy: low cost) versus that of FedEx (competitive strategy: speed). FedEx will make far more use of air transport (fast but costly) than Wal-Mart and its use of sea, truck, and rail transport.

Mini-Case: McDonald's in Russia

During the 1980s, McDonald's decided to open a facility in Moscow. McDonald's competitive strategy is low cost and conformance quality. In other words, McDonald's hamburgers taste the same anywhere you go in the world. In order to meet this goal of conformance quality and low cost, McDonald's was faced with several supply chain problems. Russia's road and rail network is extremely limited. Winston Churchill stated in the 1950s that there were no roads in Russia, only spaces between buildings. There was truth to that statement still in the 1980s. Thus, if McDonald's wanted to ship products into Moscow they would be forced to use airfreight, which did not support their low cost strategy. In addition, they could not purchase the foodstuffs locally, because the wheat, beef, cheese, and tomatoes (among others) did not meet their guidelines. Their final solution was to spend nearly 10 years building their own local supply chain. They went outside Moscow and built a ranch and farm. There they raised their own beef (so that the meat would taste the same), their own wheat (so the buns would taste the same), and their own vegetables. In this fashion, their supply chain matched their competitive strategy.

Managing a Supply Chain Strategy

As can be seen, developing a supply chain strategy requires the ability to plan for all factors that may affect you, your suppliers, and your customers. Strategy is the unique position a company seeks to occupy in its industry. The supply chain must be designed to adapt to business activities and changing circumstances, as well as the goals that the business wants to achieve. Strategic change for any business, product, or supply chain can come in the form of revolution (radical change) or evolution (continuous improvement) and the firm must consider which it is undergoing when choosing its supply chain strategy.

The three key elements of managing a supply chain strategy are:

1. focus on the customer;
2. match product type with the supply chain; and
3. include uncertainty and variability.

Focus on the Customer

What does your customer want? Customer service starts and ends with the customer because lost customer goodwill equates to lost sales. Remember that what a customer says they want and what they actually want can be two different things. Good supply chain managers must also be careful that their own mental models do not cloud the analysis of what a customer wants. Every person's previous experience, training, and beliefs impact the data they see. This can lead to distortion. As a simplistic example, if we were to ask you what the basic reason is that people buy a car, you might answer that it is transportation. What are the different motivations for people who purchase a Honda Civic, a Chrysler Minivan, a Ford F150 truck, or a Mercedes 560 SL? Applying this same concept to supply chain may mean that instead of having three deliveries a week from you (a basic concept of JIT), a customer would prefer one a week but with 100% accuracy and a 10% discount. The following is a series of questions that supply managers should ask concerning their customers.

- How much do you know about your existing customers, such as:
  - demographics
  - existing and potential number
  - income levels
- Who are your potential customers?
- How might your current and potential customers be grouped or segmented?

- What percentage of sales does each group contribute?
- What are the preferred methods of communication for each of your customers (i.e., telephone, fax, e-mail, web, Facebook, Twitter, etc.)?
- What do your customers expect from you?
- How well do your competitors meet customers' needs?

Match Product Type with the Supply Chain

Know yourself. The supply chain manager should understand the products and their production process and how well they fit together strategically. The following should be keenly understood as key components of supply chain strategy:

- Process flow
  - Linear flow
  - Job shop—batch flow
  - Assembly line
  - Continuous flow
  - Project flow
- Order fulfillment strategy
  - Make-to-order (e.g., Subway Restaurants)
  - Make-to-stock (e.g., McDonald's)

Include Uncertainty and Variability

There is not a single stage in the supply chain in which uncertainty and variability are not factors. The prudent supply chain manager must plan accordingly. Some ways to plan for uncertainty and variability are to collect statistical data on your suppliers, the manufacturing process, and your customers, and use that information to create a system that is able to withstand the expected variations.

Forecasting is an unavoidable source of uncertainty and variability. Yet it must be done in order to estimate customer demand in order to fulfill customer expectations. Forecast uncertainty can come from three places within the supply chain:

1. Suppliers
2. Manufacturing processes
3. Customer demand

The uncertainty in customer demand can be measured through metrics such as average demand and the variability of the demand.

To decrease the uncertainty in the cycle, you can:

1. use advanced analytical techniques to forecast demand;
2. adopt reliable transportation modes;
3. encourage suppliers to perform reliably;
4. stabilize manufacturing processes.

Supply chain analysis is possible with reliable data and the right quantitative techniques. Analytical and statistical methods need data, which involves a long collection process. Companies lacking current data show their carelessness toward uncertainty and ultimately toward affecting their strategies.

Additional Considerations and Types of Supply Chains

Functional versus Innovative

After the preceding items are addressed, we suggest they must be incorporated with another set of questions.

- What type of product are you producing?
- Are your products functional or are they innovative (e.g., socks vs. fashionable clothes)?

Once you have established your product type you will know whether you need a physically efficient supply chain for a functional product or whether you will need a responsive supply chain for an innovative product.

A supply chain strategy should consider the nature of the demand and the products. Products based on their demand fall into two main categories:

1. **Functional**—satisfy basic needs, do not change over time, and have stable predictable demands with long life cycles. But they lead to lower profit margins (e.g., commodity items such as socks).
2. **Innovative**—offer higher profit margins but the demands are unpredictable and their life cycles are short. For example, the clothing market for young women's clothes fluctuate based upon factors such as what Britney Spears wore in her latest music video.

Companies first need to determine whether their products are functional or innovative. Then decide whether their supply chain is physically efficient or responsive to the market because each of these products requires a different supply chain.

Supply chains perform two functions and incur costs specifically associated with each

1. **Physical**—converts raw materials into finished goods
2. **Market mediation**—tries to match the supply with the demand.

For functional products, market mediation is simple due to their nature as a commodity (i.e., socks) and physical costs need to be minimized. For a company with functional products, the goal is physical efficiency that increases productivity and reduces costs along the entire supply chain. Thus, functional products require an efficient supply chain.

The root cause of problems in many supply chains is the misalignment between the supply and the product strategies. Many companies shift from functional to innovative products but leave their supply chains as physically efficient, thereby leading to a number of broken links in its supply chain. Innovative products require a supply chain that is no longer solely focused on physical efficiency, but rather should be designed to be responsive so that it supports the new product and its markets.

When a company has an unresponsive supply chain for innovative products, the right solution is to make some of the products functional and to create a responsive supply chain for the remaining products. It is important that manufacturers and retailers work together to cut costs throughout the system, especially in the case of functional products which are highly price-sensitive. Uncertainty is inherent in innovative products and companies can reduce, avoid, or hedge uncertainties in their system.

Mass customization is a technique that can be used to create a responsive supply chain for innovative products. This is the concept of producing products to order but in lot sizes of one. Dell computers are one of the best examples of mass customization. While there are numerous ways to design a Dell computer, it is difficult to know what the customer will demand without listening to that customer. Dell began by configuring computers based on the specific demands of its customers rather than pushing products on them.

Decentralization Versus Centralization

Another factor to consider when structuring your logistics and supply chain network is that every structure is a variant of the extremes of being centralized or decentralized. Both extremes have advantages. The key is to focus on the needs of your particular firm and its strategic position. Your supply chain structure should follow from that.

Centralized supply chains are managed globally and are streamlined across all of a company's locations, divisions, brands, or both. For example, a single purchasing department, usually staffed and managed by the corporate office, can accomplish purchasing for multiple divisions. Purchasing can be the only centralized activity within a supply chain, or it can represent just one aspect of a fully centralized supply chain.

Advantages of centralization include:

- Risk pooling/Variance reduction effect
- Economies of scale
- Economies of scope
- Learning/Experience curve
- Coordination advantages
- Relationship coordination
- Smaller number of relationships
- Limited number of legal contracts.

Decentralized supply chain structures are managed at the business unit level. There are situations when organizational requirements necessitate a decentralized supply chain. For example, required or desired information or material flows may present barriers to the implementation of a centralized system. Additionally, materials and other inventories have different meanings and levels of importance to different business units that may necessitate a different type of supply chain. For example, some business units may need to order in many small quantities to support their strategy for a raw material (perhaps they are even limited on storage space) while other business units may require infrequent large deliveries of the same item. In the first case, the business unit may want to purchase items locally to facilitate the small frequent deliveries, whereas in the second case, the business unit may be able to purchase from foreign suppliers to reduce the cost of the raw material.

Advantages of decentralization include:

- Product/Process improvements
  - Proximity to suppliers
- Customer satisfaction
  - Proximity to markets/customers
- Cost savings
  - Sourcing, production, and logistics
  - Financing
- Risk diversification/Portfolio effect
  - Technology risk
  - Financial risk

Short List of Practical Considerations

A good manager must remember that every situation is unique. While you can and should learn from what other companies are doing, each firm has its own unique set of characteristics that impact every managerial decision. This list is a compilation of practical considerations that each manager should keep in mind. They are general issues so that they can provide general guidance in a broad array of situations and companies.

- Logistics is the natural link between Operations and Marketing to make more efficient the flow of goods and information along the logistics system. Optimization of individual linkages does not guarantee global solutions and that is why you need a Global Logistics Approach, for example, Resource Oriented Logistics, User Oriented Logistics, Information Oriented Logistics.

- Outsourcing is a great alternative for rationalizing the existing resources of a company, however, do not outsource without analyzing the strategic fit with the core competence, for example, strategic role of the part in isolation versus strategic role of the part to final assembly.

- Third Party Logistics (3PL) companies are excellent alternatives for outsourcing logistics; however, make sure the needs as well as the specific measurement is determined in advance. If you don't specify upfront how the performance will be monitored and measured, in our experience, you will be disappointed by the lack of "transparency" in the service you receive.

- The strategy drives the requirements for a better understanding and management of the logistics and supply chain system. The best alliances are the ones where your strategic requirements mesh with those of your partner.

Key Take-Aways

- Strategic alliances are necessary for global operations. They come in many different forms and types depending on the needs of your organization. SCM depends on relationship building and, as such, supply chain relationships should be considered strategically and not just be based on low costs or convenience.

- Outsourcing is a strategy that can provide competitive advantages to your organization, if managed properly. Outsourcing decisions should be made with cross-functional teams and considered as part of the overall business strategy versus being reviewed in isolation.

- Again, we see the importance of integration and coordination within the supply chain. The best laid plans for ensuring integration and coordination still fail when they do not ensure that the implemented processes are maintained and audit them from time to time to ensure that the processes are still serving the needs of the organization.
- Strategy comes in two versions: cost or differentiation.
- Differentiation can be created through quality, flexibility, speed, or both.
- The three key elements of managing a supply chain strategy are:
  1. Focus on the customer
  2. Match product type with the supply chain
  3. Include uncertainty and variability
- Determine the type of supply chain that best suits your company, products, and customers.
  1. Functional versus innovative
  2. Centralized versus decentralized

Reflection Points

1. How have you utilized strategic alliances within your firm? Were you happy with the results? How well does your company manage strategic alliances that demand that multiple departments within your organization interact with your strategic partner? How are these types of complex relationships managed within your organization?

2. What outsourcing opportunities does your organization have available? Is the company taking advantage of these opportunities? Why or why not? What are your competitors outsourcing? Has your firm ever considered bringing functions back inhouse that have been outsourced? Are there any functions now that should be considered for bringing back inhouse?

3. What is the competitive strategy of your firm? Has your competitive strategy been challenged by competitive issues, a changing environment, or even yourself?

4. Does your firm's supply chain strategy support the firm's competitive strategy?

5. How do your firm's customers benefit from your supply chain strategy?

6. Does your firm have more than one supply chain and supply chain strategy? Do you think this is feasible?

7. What benefits could your company enjoy by centralizing or decentralizing functions within the supply chain?

8. When was the last time that someone challenged the status quo of your purchasing methodologies?

Additional Resources

Dobosz, A., & Dougal, A. (2012, May/June). Releasing supply chain value. *Supply Chain Solutions 42*(3), 72–74.

Lee, H. L., & Billington, C. (1993, September). Material management in decentralized supply chains. *Operations Research 41*(5), 835–847.

Muzumdar, M., & Balachandran, N. (2001, October). The supply chain evolution: Roles, responsibilities, and implications for management. *APICS the Performance Advantage.*

SECTION 2

SCM Components

CHAPTER 4

Forecasting

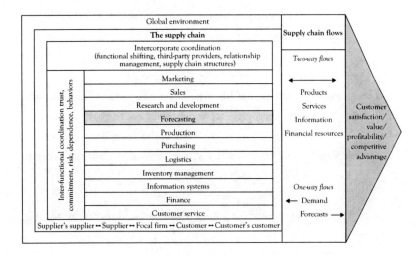

Chapter Objectives

- Introduce forecasting methods
- Explore the facets of forecast and their dynamic nature
- Discuss how forecasts can be optimized
- Explore types of future outlooks
- Consider forecasting best practices
- Apply forecasting in a mini-case

In order to survive in today's competitive markets, the forecasting process must be mastered. We introduce you to the five points of view a fore-caster can have of the future and describe particularities in international forecasting. In addition, this chapter shows benchmarks in the forecasting process, the models used, and the applied software solutions and systems. Finally, a best practice solution is presented along with emergent phe-nomena that show the trend for forecasting in the future.

Forecasting Methods

There are four basic forecasting methodologies defined by Chopra and Meindl at Northwestern University:[1]

Qualitative: Forecasting based on personal insight or intuition.

Causal: This assumes that specific variables drive the forecast. For example, interest rate increases by the Federal Reserve may decrease commercial loan activity. Or, your customer is opening 25 new stores, which will increase your sales to that customer.

Time series: Assumes that historical data will predict future trends. For example, some companies forecast sales each month based on the sales at the same time last year.

Simulation: Combines causal and time series methods in order to try out what-if scenarios.

Most companies use a combination of these techniques to create their forecasts.

Key Concepts in Forecasting

Forecasting is more accurate for short time frames than when used for long-term planning. For example, when Wal-Mart had their stores begin ordering every two weeks rather than each month, inventories were reduced because forecasting accuracy increased. Different forecasting tools are applicable for different applications and time frames. The table on the next page provides a basic comparison of the types of forecasts routinely done by organizations.

Additionally, there are five concepts that must always be taken into account when planning for the future. These are:

- **Impact of technology:** If, in the 1970s, you were the CEO of Smith Corona typewriters and had not considered the impact of PCs on your business, you would have been blown out of the water (which is exactly what happened).

Application	Short Term (0–3 Months)	Medium Term (3 Months–2 Years)	Long Term (more than 2 Years)
Forecast quantity	Individual products or services	Total sales groups, or families of products or services	Total sales
Decision area	Inventory management, final assembly scheduling, workforce scheduling, master production scheduling	Staff planning, production planning, master production scheduling, purchasing distribution	Facility location, capacity planning, process management
Forecasting technique	Time series, causal, qualitative	Time series, causal, qualitative	Causal, qualitative, simulation

- **Social issues:** For example, microwave ovens were available in the 1950s but the market was not there since most women were not working outside the home.
- **Political issues:** For example, when governments offered subsidies for development of new products, this caused accelerated product introduction. Hybrid vehicles in California are one such example.
- **Legal issues:** The federal breakup of Bell Telephone significantly impacted the rate at which new products and services were offered by the phone company(s).
- **Environmental issues:** For example, the demand for cleaner air can drive the development of new technologies and services. And, wide open spaces such as in Dallas, TX do not pressure the population to make use of services such as mass transit like citizens in Boston, MA who are forced to take advantage of their mass transit system due to the city's significant population density and limited space due to the adjacent harbor.

Given the importance of forecasting, it is often perplexing to see that companies have no centralized structure in place to ensure data capture and accuracy. Without appropriate and accurate data, forecasts are not reliable. Often, different divisions within the same company use different methods, software, and databases to forecast creating *isolated islands of information.*

Meanwhile, overall company forecasts are difficult to construct and have reduced accuracy because the various software packages and databases are not compatible. This is a classic example of what can happen when companies focus on business functions rather than business processes.

This is another case of not speaking the same language that builds walls between functions, departments, and team members.

Breakthroughs in technology make it possible for companies to gather relevant information more readily than in the past. Yet, many companies are caught in the traditional *functionalist syndrome* that continues to perpetuate departmental forecasts—creating forecasts that are not fully integrated into an overall aggregate plan fitted to the prevailing corporate strategy.

Forecast Optimization

To optimize the process of forecasting, business units have to:

- collaborate with internal departments and partners outside the company;
- have the capacity to integrate its suppliers and customers into its forecasting processes;
- be proactive in becoming involved in programs like VMI (Vendor Managed Inventory) and CPFR (Collaborative Planning, Forecasting, and Replenishment).
- assign accountability, and mean it!
- ensure that all parties involved in forecasting are using the same "language" and understand each other's concerns, contributions, and expectations;
- allow the forecast to be wrong—no one can predict the future 100% correctly. Don't let fear of being wrong bog down the process;
- continually improve the forecasting process—don't settle for *good enough*!

In the past, companies have mainly forecasted intuitively based on managerial insights, experience, and instincts. In recent years, however, companies favor scientific approaches that are based on facts and data. Each department has to forecast its business for the upcoming period to optimize the overall performance of the company. Technology enables the storage of large amounts of data in data warehouses. Forecasting software and processes apply models that can improve precision of forecasts.

Five Viewpoints of the Future

The viewpoints of supply chain managers determine the selection of forecasting information. It is imperative to back up forecasts with both logical and credible data, but credibility varies depending on the audience and situation. As a consequence, some thought should be given in determining what angle to seek when choosing forecasting methods, based on the decision maker's viewpoints of the future. There are five basic categories to which these viewpoints can be classified to help determine adequate forecasting methods. They are extrapolators, pattern analysts, goal analysts, counter-punchers, and intuitors. The key is to realize that none of these viewpoints alone is perfect for every situation, but the right combination of these viewpoints and their techniques will produce the most valid information for supply chain managers.

Extrapolators

Extrapolators fall into the quantitative category when it comes to the type of data that they value and utilize for creating forecasts. Their basic belief is that the future is reasonably predictable, based on past trends. One weakness of this belief is that it fails to take dramatic changes into consideration that could occur in the present but are not considered in the past data. Engineers usually follow this viewpoint on the future. Common techniques and methods used are:

- Trend Extrapolation
- Fisher–Pry Substitution Analysis
- Gompertz Substitution Analysis

- Growth Limit Analysis
- Learning Curves

Pattern Analysts

Pattern analysts also value quantitative information and are very similar to extrapolators. They basically believe that history repeats itself and that one may forecast the future by identifying and analyzing situations from the past and applying the cycles to future circumstances. A good example of a pattern analyst is a pure scientist. Common techniques and methods used are:

- Analog Analysis
- Precursor Trend Analysis
- Morphological Analysis
- Feedback Models

Goal Analysts

Goal analysts rely less on quantitative data and more on the belief that the future is determined by the actions and beliefs of a collection of individuals, organizations, and institutions. Their basis of forecasting is determining the goals of trendsetters and supply chain mangers, and figuring out how large of an impact they can have on future trends. Individuals in marketing are usually goal analysts. This thinking takes on a more real-world approach but also does not emphasize the importance of other forces that impact change. Forecasting methods and techniques commonly used are:

- Impact Analysis
- Content Analysis
- Stakeholder Analysis
- Patent Analysis

Counter-Punchers

Counter-punchers are on the qualitative side of the spectrum when it comes to the data that they use in forecasting. Their belief is that the future is a result of random events and the best way to stay in tune is to follow trends and plan accordingly. There is a high degree of judgment used in this type of forecast. Typical counter-punchers are usually executives. Common techniques and methods used are:

- Scanning, Monitoring, and Tracking
- Alternate Scenarios
- Cross-Impact Analysis

Intuitors

Finally, intuitors believe that a mixture of driving forces, random events, and the actions of key individuals and institutions shapes the future. The world is too complex to use a rational technique to project the future, so one should gather all the data available and use personal intuition to make forecasts. Intuitors are usually executives, as well. Their common techniques and methods are:

- Delphi Surveys
- Nominal Group Analysis
- Structured and Unstructured Interviews

Levels of Forecasting

Forecasting is one important part of company achievement. One must know the number of products the customers want. However, world trading is changing to a global supply and demand chain. Knowing local customers and doing organizational forecasting is not enough. Companies must carry on international forecasting, as well.

Organizational Forecasting

The main factors affecting accuracy on this level are:

- Sales and marketing involvement
- Software design procedures

- Forecasting team structure
- Data input
- Parameter setting
- Sales and operation planning

Top-Down Approach

The top-down approach is common and simple because companies forecast on an aggregate level by using basic inputs such as historical data and promotion effects. It is suitable for predictable sales trends. However, management sometimes biases forecasting results because they are trying to meet sales targets.

Bottom-Up Approach

The bottom-up approach is more complex than the first one. There are larger numbers of forecasters involved. Sales representatives or local officers usually forecast at a local level. The approach is proper for specific promotional products and effective in planning for warehousing, manufacturing and transportation. The disadvantage is that lower level historical data is usually lost or not completed.

International Level

All factors mentioned in the organizational level forecast still have an effect on forecasting results, but cultural differences among regions will be another important factor. For example, Latin American cultures prefer bright and vibrant colors while Asians do not. Also, Americans prefer sweeter foods than Europeans do. Therefore, when companies engage in international forecasting, culture cannot be overlooked.

Best Practices in Forecasting

Among forecasting functions, people, process, technology, and resources, the forecasting process itself is the most important factor in creating an accurate forecast. The process connects people to technology and resources. Because all departments of a company have to be involved in the forecasting process it is essential to coordinate and synchronize actions.

To take full advantage a company has to synchronize forecast period and lead time. To make the forecast as precise as possible, forecasted and actual results have to be monitored and compared carefully. In an ever-changing business environment, companies have to make sure that their forecasting process still meets market realities.

Forecasting is essential in any fast-moving sector where demand or product mix changes. Experience over the last few decades of commercial forecasting has identified good practices, which improve the likelihood of providing effective forecasting. A good forecast should be timely, accurate, reliable, made in meaningful units for the users, simple to understand, and *documented in a way that enables later review*.

For a good forecast…

- focus on short-range forecasts, as these are the drivers of immediate sales and replenishment activities;
- forecast at a product family level wherever possible, as this will be more accurate than the individual stock-keeping unit (SKU) level;
- understand the business well, utilize cross-functional teams, ask your customer about their forecasting techniques and how to integrate their information into your process.
- the original forecasts should be retained and regularly measured for errors using various types of auditing techniques;
- a good forecasting software should be used that will provide an easy to use and visual interface as well as good forecasting tools;
- source data should be used for historical information, be careful not to use information that has been aggregated in such a way that it hinders your forecast;
- capture and use as much source data as you can, involve your IT department, let them know what you need—don't be satisfied with what they say is available, if you need more.

Mini-Case: Why Supply Chain Forecasting
Is a Best Practice at HP

At HP merged with Compaq, managers needed simple and consistent supply chain models for the combined businesses. They knew they had to identify the best practices in each organization and apply them to the merged operations. The management used a wide range of communication techniques, supported by computing infrastructure, in order to find large savings for the combined operations. The parties agreed on common business tools and published their choice so that it was available for other members of the organization. At every node of the supply chain, a consensus forecast confronts net demand and supply. As a consequence, a detailed communication flow was provided for all members of the supply chain. The forecast of demand is updated on a daily basis. If a plan changes, the reason has to be explained to the supply chain partners. HP uses SAP's Enterprise Resource Planning software and uses the Internet to distribute a daily action plan, based on the demand forecast to all the impacted members of the supply chain. HP's Ink Jet division cut its forecasting time for the supply cycle by three days. The Enterprise Server Group business unit has shortened the change order process from three weeks to just 24 hours. Through all their measures, HP continuously increased the efficiency of its operations and enhanced its customer satisfaction.

Key Take-Aways

- In a dynamic and global market place, rules of the game change rapidly due to factors such as uncertainty in demand, changes in technology, and changes in competition.
- Business forecasters attempt to control the demand uncertainties by using various forecasting techniques also by using a fair amount of insights, judgment, and intuition.
- Forecasting may be done at the individual, organizational, and international levels.
  - At an individual level, customer tastes and preferences are considered.

- ○ The organizational level will include the aggregated data on consumers, advertising effects, and economic trends.
- ○ Analysis at the international level may focus on cultural differences between countries in terms of power–distance, uncertainty avoidance, individualism/collectivism, and masculinity/femininity.
- Any business problem or opportunity requires valid forecasts, which should start with defining the objectives of the forecast.
- Various techniques may be selected from different views since the validity of the forecast will depend on the breadth of techniques used.
- Fight functionalist syndrome and watch the accuracy of your forecasts increase.

Reflection Points

1. Does your company have "functionalist syndrome"? If so, what can you, your team, or both of you, do to improve integration and cooperation using technology? What other methods could you use to improve forecasting in your company?
2. What approach does your company take to forecasting? Is the approach taken, the same one, throughout the organization?
3. What type of quality control do you have in place in order to insure that your forecasts are meeting the needs of the organization?
4. As a leader, do you understand the forecasting process in your company? Truly understand how it was developed, how it works, and if it is being changed to meet the needs of the organization as required?

Additional Resources

Bonabeu, E. (2002). Predicting the unpredictable. *Harvard Business Review* *80*(3). 5–11.

Hammond, J. H., Obermayer, W. R. (1994). Making supply meet demand in an uncertain world. *Harvard Business Review 72*(3), 83–93.

Jain, C. L. (2003, Fall). Business forecasting in the 21st century. *The Journal of Business Forecasting* 3–6.

CHAPTER 5

Inventory Management

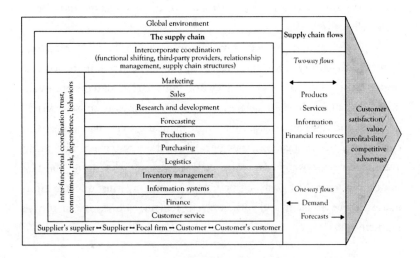

Chapter Objectives

- Define inventory management
- Explore the implications of inventory management to the firm
- Discuss the tools and techniques used in inventory management
- Explore factors that directly affect inventory management
- Focus on practice
- Applied inventory management review using mini-cases
- Examine trends in inventory management
- Learn from an Economic Order Quantity example

It is important for a company to successfully manage its inventory using all the techniques that it has available and those the firm sees fit for its type of business. By doing this the company can lower costs such as overhead and increase customer satisfaction by improving inventory availability. Both *physical* and *logical* inventories require accurate and up-to-date information in order to be managed adequately. Carrying the right amount of inventory and ensuring that neither overstocking nor shortages occur is the ultimate goal of inventory management. Strong inventory control is also dependent on accurate forecasts and timely replenishments.

Managed and organized information leads to better forecasting, improved inventory turns, lower costs, system efficiencies, increased customer satisfaction, and the list goes on. Information systems are established and maintained in a variety of ways. A company must ascertain its needs and develop or acquire an information system that supports its current and future business strategies. While these systems can be costly, a company must weigh the costs and benefits and determine the best solution to meet their goals. Nonetheless, a company must manage information to be efficient and ultimately to remain competitive in today's marketplace.

A Little History

It has been said that war brings with it atrocities, however, sometimes great progress is achieved out of the mechanics of war. World War II was the principal creator of the science of operations research (OR). OR development began in the United Kingdom and later spilled over to the United States, where, in the early 1950s industrial operations management and research grew. With this growth, inventory policies took center stage in organizations due to inter- and intradepartmental complexities such as the following:

- The production department strove for efficiency, which demanded uninterrupted production runs, which meant a large inventory of work in process, as well as finished goods.
- Marketing wanted to provide customers with immediate delivery of goods, therefore demanded a large and diverse inventory.

- Finance wanted to minimize inventory balances in order to reduce capital blockage and to stabilize labor, which required goods to be produced for inventory at slack periods.

These issues gave rise to a major question: *What inventory policy is best for the organization?*

To address such questions, organizations needed a way to balance their overall business strategy as well as the objectives of individual departments. This need gave birth to the science of **inventory management**, a process to optimize the production and movement of raw materials, semifinished and finished products while meeting the financial and economic requirements of the firm.

Solutions to deal with problems of inventory management were developed as far back as 1915 by F. W. Harris. He developed the economic-lot-size equation. This equation sought to minimize the sum of inventory carrying cost and setup cost related to production and inventory control, when demands were certain. It was only in the early 1960s, however, that concepts such as inventory forecasting and safety stock were introduced to help deal with fluctuating demands.

What Is Inventory Management?

Inventory Management encompasses processes that ensure product availability while reducing investment costs. For most companies, there are two forms of inventory:

- **Physical inventory:** includes all the materials that are tangible and required to fabricate the final product. Physical inventory also includes the final product, including final packout materials.
- **Logical inventory:** includes databases, inventory-tracking software, and other such intangible information-based assets.

Proper synchronization of these two inventories is essential for proper management of company assets. Inventory management also involves identifying the most effective source of supply for each item in each stocking location. Forecasting and replenishment are also integral components that facilitate inventory management.

Why Do We Need Inventory Management?

Inventory is the **largest** (we mean in the physical and financial sense of the word "large") and most difficult asset to manage for any organization. Improper management of inventory may lead to:

- **Overstocking:** Excess inventory can lead to increased costs, capital intensity, and potential obsolescence of stock ultimately reducing the *flexibility* and *profitability* of the firm.
- **Shortages:** It is possible that some items are not available to be shipped in a timely manner to meet the customer's order requirements; this is considered an inventory shortage. In some cases, the inventory may be available but not traceable because of poor information control, availability, or both. In either case, the organization risks disappointing the customer and potentially damaging its reputation, breaching contractual obligations or, worst case, permanently losing a customer.
- **Inaccurate information in logical inventory:** This inaccuracy can lead to inaccurate forecasting, as well as not being able to locate inventory that is actually available, overstocked, or in shortage of any type of inventory: raw materials, work-in-process, and finished goods.
- **Unsatisfactory return on investment (ROI):** The inventory holding costs may overshadow any profits earned.
- **Reductions in working capital:** By holding slow-moving inventory companies tie up working capital and lengthen their cash-to-cash conversion cycle. This reduction and inhibition of cash flow can affect the company's ability to finance capital expenses, make debt payments, and ultimately could bring a company to its proverbial knees. In many cases, bank covenants have tight restrictions built into their calculations to ensure that companies are encouraged to not carry excess inventories.

How Does Inventory Management Help Us?

The following are benefits of proper management of inventory:

- **Better forecasting:** Accurate inventory information improves forecasting capabilities. This in turn can improve customer service and can reduce instances of overstocking or shortages.
- **Improved financial returns by reducing costs:** Inventory control activities are costly. Properly managed inventory reduces these costs. There are several different financial costs involved:
  - Cost of stocking and distributing materials
  - Rent and utility expenses of warehouse
  - Insurance and taxes on physical inventory
  - Capital invested in inventory.
- **Identification of crucial products:** Better management can help differentiate between types of inventory items based on importance, customer category, and so forth.
- **Ability to Support JIT:** Properly managed inventory is essentially the same as having a JIT inventory process.

Factors Affecting Inventory Management

Despite the extensive coverage afforded to asset decisions in financial management literature and education, there tends to be one glaring shortcoming—inventory management is overlooked. The management of cash, physical capital assets, and, to a somewhat lesser extent, receivables are dealt with extensively. Claiming that inventory is a relatively insignificant asset cannot defend this omission. On the contrary, even in this time of service industry domination, inventory management has important ramifications within any economy.

There are some major factors that have an impact on the management of inventory. Some of these overlooked factors are cost, order size, forecasting, capacity planning and production scheduling.

Cost

Commodity prices can vary dramatically over a relatively short period of time. A strong expectation of rising prices could lead to an immediate, above-normal inventory buildup of the affected raw material. On the other hand, a strong expectation of falling prices might lead to an above-normal inventory stock reduction. A purchasing manager should compare the incremental carrying costs of larger inventory stocks to the expected price increase. The probability of error in all price expectations must, of course, also be kept in mind.

Order Size

There are various costs incurred each time an order is placed with a manufacturer, including delivery charges, handling costs, and paperwork expenses. It behooves a distributor to minimize the frequency of placing orders in order to hold down ordering costs. However, infrequent ordering necessitates large order sizes, thereby leading to greater inventory stocks and an increase in carrying costs. Manufacturing firms also place orders for goods, particularly raw materials, and parts for use in production. By placing large orders, a manufacturer can, in essence, utilize inventory to minimize ordering costs. But again, inventory-carrying costs must be incorporated into such a decision. It is the *tradeoff* between ordering cost and carrying cost.

Forecasting

The forecasting function seeks to predict future demand. Forecasting is important in determining capacity, tooling, and personnel requirements. There are two types of forecasting, long-range and-short range, each supporting different components of the overall business strategy.

Capacity Planning

Capacity planning is critical to production planning. Demands have to be anticipated: How far into the future should we go? The size of the capacity increment depends on the flexibility of the equipment we choose: Should we add capacity by expanding an existing facility, or should we build/buy/lease a new one? It is often more expensive to build a new facility then to expand an existing one, but a new facility can often lead to other efficiencies. Again there are many tradeoffs that must be considered.

Production Scheduling

Production planning is another key element in the inventory management process. Continuous process manufacturers often produce a mix of products, one at a time, using the same equipment and facilities. Each time a different product is to be produced, it is necessary to stop the production process and make adjustments before proceeding. The costs of shutdown and adjustments, which are referred to as changeover costs, can be high. Production time is lost while the facilities are closed down, and labor costs must be expended to make the necessary adjustments. As a consequence of the changeover costs, businesses try to find ways to minimize the number of changeovers. One of the ways of achieving this goal is through the use of inventory management. Simply put, a company can choose to make many short production runs on each product in the mix, thereby incurring many changeovers and having smaller lots in inventory, or it can opt for long production runs and very few changeovers and increasing inventory lots. The Economic Order Quantity (EOQ) model helps managers find the breakeven point for this situation.

Tools and Techniques of Inventory Management

There are many mathematical models for inventory control that can be used to determine the best strategy for inventory management. Some of oldest and simplest models include Economic Order Quantity (EOQ) and Wagner–Whitin Procedure. Today, most of the industries are using techniques like Manufacturing Resource Planning (MRP II), Just in Time (JIT), or Enterprise Resource Planning (ERP), which is the next-generation MRP II.

1. The **Economic Order Quantity** (EOQ) model is the order quantity at which the combination of ordering costs and inventory carrying costs is minimized. It is the most cost-effective quantity to purchase or produce for each replenishment. The EOQ model is applicable if demand for an item has a *constant rate* and the *entire quantity ordered arrives in inventory at one point in time*. The EOQ equation and problem set are provided at the end of this chapter.

○ Production, purchasing, and inventory managers frequently use EOQ calculations in business. This tool provides everything it takes to make reliable calculations. In addition, EOQ automatically computes the reorder point (the inventory level at which new orders must be placed) and order cycle time, including consideration for any applicable lead times or safety stock requirements.

2. The **Wagner–Whitin Procedure** assumes deterministic demand and deterministic production. It is better suited for purchasing than a production system.

3. **Manufacturing Resource Planning II** is used in many industries. MRP II is a computational system that utilizes data management through an integrated information system. Planning and scheduling is based upon historical data, forecasts, system constraints, and other such variables. Use of manufacturing resource planning in conjunction with product Bills of Materials (BOMs) can forecast materials requirements on a lot basis—known as Material Requirements Planning.

4. **Enterprise Resource Planning** (ERP) combines all departmental information together into a single, integrated information system so that the various departments can easily share information and communicate with each other. This integrated approach of centralized databases reduces duplicate or conflicting information, or both, caused when departments are responsible for "islands of information" that are not interconnected within the organization.

5. **Just in Time** (JIT) inventory, as the title indicates, works on a real time working environment basis. It assumes zero defects, small lot sizes, reduce setups and breakdowns, as well as minimal lead times. The goal of JIT is to reduce in process inventory and the carrying costs associated with increased inventories.

In most manufacturing systems, a small fraction of purchased parts represents the largest portion of the firm's purchasing expenditures. In order to differentiate parts based on importance and requirements, many firms use an **ABC Classification** system to identify purchased parts and materials. Items classified as "A" category parts make up generally

5 to 10% of the individual parts yet collectively account for 75 to 80% of total annual expenditures or unit movement. "B" category parts represent the next 10 to 15% and generally account for 10 to 15% of total annual expenditures or unit movement. "C" category items represent the bottom 80% and account for only 10% of total annual expenditures or unit movement.

These are some of the techniques used for inventory control management, however, in today's world ERP (which can include MRP) and JIT tend to be the most widely used.

Focus on Practice

Conversion to JIT

As a matter of practice and implementation, there are many firms that have used MRP for years, however, because of upper management pressure, they are now moving to JIT. This brings up the issue of how to move employees and production systems from an MRP environment that has become ingrained in the corporate culture to something new. The simplest approach is to continue to use MRP, but move from large fixed-order quantities to smaller quantities, the goal being a lot size of 1. Continue this process until you have moved all MRP lots to a Lot for Lot (LFL) strategy, which is the same as a lot size of 1. After LFL has been used for a period of time, congratulate your employees on their embracing of JIT concepts (which is basically what they have been doing). At this point, it is much easier to transition to a true JIT environment, than an all-or-nothing or "cold turkey" approach.

Intensification in Inventory Management Use

Retailers continue looking for an optimal blend of art and science to conduct inventory management activities. They have spent time, money, and resources instituting fundamental techniques, establishing inventory control, and aligning their assortments. The marketplace continues to become increasingly competitive and executing the basics compared with rivals may no longer be enough. For that reason, more inventory management techniques and practices are being used and the number is expected to grow. This growth is corroborated in a survey performed by

Bearingpoint Inc. in 2003 on retail industries in the United States including department, big box, specialty, drug, and home improvement stores.[1] They found that 51% of the participants generate more than $500 million or more in annual sales and operate 100 stores or more.

In the survey, respondents showed that communications and shared information between retailers and their vendor partners had increased by 18% over 2002. This is seen in the following chart.

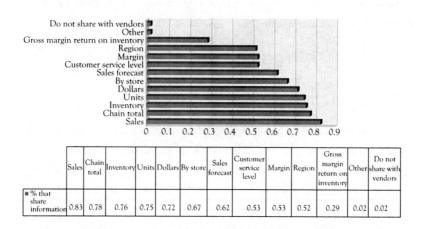

	Sales	Chain total	Inventory	Units	Dollars	By store	Sales forecast	Customer service level	Margin	Region	Gross margin return on inventory	Other	Do not share with vendors
■ % that share information	0.83	0.78	0.76	0.75	0.72	0.67	0.62	0.53	0.53	0.52	0.29	0.02	0.02

The percentage of companies that shared inventory information was 76%. The three most used methods of sharing information and managing product inventory were *category management* (management of product categories as strategic business units), *automatic replenishment*, and *model stock level* with 67, 61, and 59% respectively as shown in the following chart.

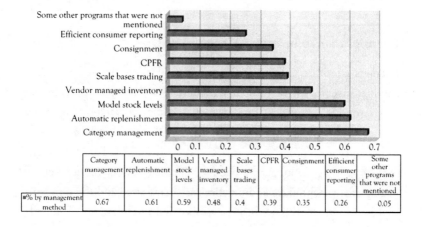

	Category management	Automatic replenishment	Model stock levels	Vendor managed inventory	Scale bases trading	CPFR	Consignment	Efficient consumer reporting	Some other programs that were not mentioned
■% by management method	0.67	0.61	0.59	0.48	0.4	0.39	0.35	0.26	0.05

Major obstacles faced by retailers in maintaining inventory integrity were rated by each organization on a scale from 1 to 10 (rating of 10 signifies as "extremely dramatic impact"). The result was that the three major obstacles were identified: receiving, selling, and physical inventory counting errors, all with values of more than 6.5. This is shown in the next chart.

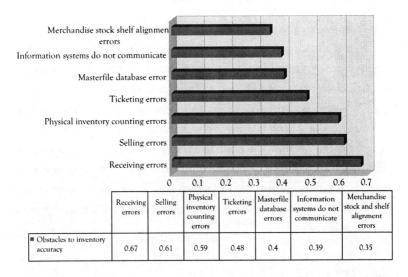

	Receiving errors	Selling errors	Physical inventory counting errors	Ticketing errors	Masterfile database errors	Information systems do not communicate	Merchandise stock and shelf alignment errors
▓ Obstacles to inventory accuracy	0.67	0.61	0.59	0.48	0.4	0.39	0.35

Almost all retailers agree that in order to reduce these errors they need to apply better employee training on policies and procedures, organization education, continue implementation in barcode scanning, and establishing specialty measurements in terms of accuracy as shown in the next chart.

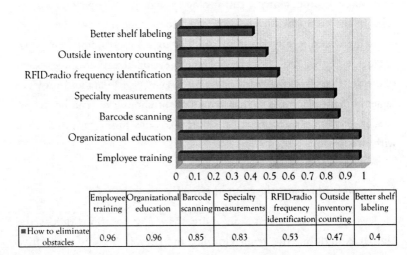

	Employee training	Organizational education	Barcode scanning	Specialty measurements	RFID-radio frequency identification	Outside inventory counting	Better shelf labeling
▓ How to eliminate obstacles	0.96	0.96	0.85	0.83	0.53	0.47	0.4

Mini-Case Examples of Implementation

Companies around the world have been successful implementing Inventory Management practices and techniques.

Wal-Mart

Wal-Mart's success is not just due to offering lower prices to the customer; it is also attributed to applying inventory management (only having in stock what people want). By electronically linking to their suppliers through electronic data interchange (EDI) and their cross-docking strategy, Wal-Mart and their suppliers gain advantages from "just-in-time" inventory control. The process is also streamlined through the elimination of paperwork from the stock reordering process, and the consequent elimination of processes associated with sorting, mailing, and storing of paper-based transactions. Wal-Mart savings have been approximately $180 million by reducing its inventory and thus the annual cost of carrying excess inventory.

Home Depot

The Home Depot formula for success is a warehouse store format that features everyday low pricing, extraordinary customer service, quality products, and a large assortment of items. Price is a critical factor and sourcing, procurement, and inventory management play important roles in the company's overall strategy. Home Depot moves over 85% of its merchandise directly from supplier to store, avoiding warehousing altogether. In addition, Home Depot developed a forecasting system internally that uses two years' of point-of-sale (POS) data and provides replenishment planning, so that inventory threshold levels can be set and vendor lead times accounted for. Home Depot's profit rose over 15% with all the improvements.

Littlewoods Stores in the United Kingdom

Littlewoods Stores operates in more than 250 locations across the United Kingdom. The retail clothing industry is highly competitive

and for that reason, Littlewoods began initiatives to improve their supply chain and specifically to deal with an overstocking problem. They
implemented a data warehouse system, DSS, and other software that
transformed the business. The results included a 20% inventory reduction, 2% increase in margins, improvements in inventory turns, a 40%
increase in staff productivity, and a 59 to 85% increase in cross-docking
efficiency.

7-Eleven

7-Eleven is the United States' number 1 convenience-store chain in rev-
enues. To compete more effectively, they rolled out an inventory management and sales data system that not only made the most of its limited
shelf space and product assortment, but also moved new products into
stores and improved its position with its supplier. Using sales and inventory data, they hand over two dozen new products to store managers
weekly including fresh and perishable food and were able to optimize
sales and improve their inventory. 7-Eleven has grown to $10 billion in
US sales and $33 billion worldwide with all improvements.

Arizona Public Service (APS)

APS is the largest utility provider in Arizona, serving 705,000 customers and generating $1.7 billion in revenues annually. APS decided to
scrutinize its supply chain for ways to increase efficiency and invest in
new technology to support management of materials and services. They
developed an electronic system that enables buyers and other company
personnel to buy products and services through the streamlined processes
of three online software modules (Material Catalog, Description Buy, and
Express Buy). The time spent on improving the supply chain permit-
ted APS to trim inventory by 25%, and reduce purchasing cost by 5%.
In turn, APS reduced the consumer electric rate by 5%.

Numerous other companies such as General Motors, Toyota (the
leader in JIT), Kmart, JCPenney, the U.S. Department of Defense, and so
on are applying inventory management to improve customer service levels,
warehouse efficiency, and overall profit. In general, American businesses

have succeeded in applying various inventory management techniques. The U.S. Department of Commerce reported that from 1981 to 2000, inventory as a percentage of GDP fell 46%, from 8.3 to 3.8%.

The greatest challenge, by far, involves getting associates in different parts of the supply chain to work together. That's because many organizations still operate in a functional cost manner, where managers are rewarded for improving performance only within their own internal group.

Trends in Inventory Control

Companies are now seeing that collaboration between suppliers and vendors is important to making the supply chain successful. This idea of working together in a healthy relationship is driving what is being developed for the future of inventory management.

Electronic Data Interchange

EDI is helping many businesses in sharing data and improving inventory control. EDI is simply a way by which companies communicate electronically via computer systems directly to one another. When companies do not have the technology necessary, there are third party vendors that provide the connectivity necessary for trading electronically. EDI has many facets. If the customer (e.g., retailer) makes inventory information available to the supplier, the supplier can utilize EDI to know when their inventory needs replenishing and can adjust the near-term manufacturing forecast plan using this information.

Additionally, when a company needs to place an order, they can do this through an EDI system and avoid a paper trail of purchase orders because the system will automatically save the information. It provides faster communication from one entity to another and companies can access real time data. Other information flows through an EDI system, as well, such as accounts receivable, returns, chargebacks, receiving, and so forth. Each EDI communication system is specific to the retailer and the vendor. This is also considered **B2B** (Business to Business) electronic communication.

Vendor Managed Inventory (VMI)

Using a VMI program, a company outsources its inventory control to their supplier. VMI works by allowing the supplier to have electronic access (usually through EDI and sometimes through web-based access) to the customer's inventory database. Suppliers can monitor the movement of the inventory through the customer (e.g., manufacturer or retailer) and can manage their own inventories, purchases, and production accordingly. VMI programs can result in inventory reduction due to the supplier handling inventory tracking and replenishment planning. Suppliers can many times receive preferred vendor status if they are able to participate in VMI. It is important to know if this is something that your customer or potential customers want to achieve. If so, as the vendor you should be prepared accordingly.

Scan-Based Trading (SBT)

SBT is mainly used by supermarkets, however, the concept is growing in popularity with retailers such as do-it-yourself (DIY) stores. Using point-of-sale information the system allows for a perpetual inventory count; when an item is scanned at checkout the computer system adjusts the inventory accordingly and transmits data to the supplier. This information is usually captured on a daily basis and transmitted by batch to the vendor each day.

The difference in this system compared to other perpetual inventory control is that the *supplier owns the inventory until the item is scanned for purchase*; ownership of the goods passes at the time of the sale to the final consumer.

At the time of sale, the title of the goods passes from the manufacturer, to the retailer, and, ultimately, to the consumer, all of which occur simultaneously. The retailer is obligated to pay for the goods, generally 7 to 10 days after the sale to the consumer (these terms are usually more favorable than the standard 30–60 day terms for other inventory). The supermarket acts like a warehouse for the manufacturer. The supplier gets real-time information on when their products are bought and can schedule their deliveries based on how much of an item remains in the store.

SBT can reduce inventories, cut labor costs, streamline distribution, and maintain the optimal amount of inventory, saving money for both the supplier and store. It should be noted that in this type of situation the burden of inventory carrying costs moves from the retailer to the manufacturer, including but not limited to shrink (loss of inventory due to damage or theft).

Collaborative Planning, Forecasting, and Replenishment (CPFR)

CPFR combines EDI and VMI. It is different because it allows more shared information between two entities and increases collaboration. It links the supply and demand of a product so that the retailer is more involved in the supply chain because both companies will be able to see the entire supply chain from one end to the other. The final retailer will be able to be involved from the manufacturing of raw materials to the final product. All the suppliers that are involved in the process of making an item are linked together and can get information about the other. This helps to determine shortcomings of material of any manufacturer in the chain so that companies can plan accordingly.

Radio Frequency Identification (RFID)

A technology that has started to emerge to help with inventory management is RFID. RFID uses a computer chip and reader to let the user know when an item has arrived at an entrance and when it leaves an exit. Wal-Mart first started to use this in 2000 for individual items but dropped the study and decided it would be better to track pallets of goods. This has been the trend in industry as of this time. Until costs are reduced substantially, RFID at the pallet level is as detailed as tracking will get within the supply chain except for high value items.

All these programs are used to keep real-time data on inventory. They are designed so that a company and its supplier will know simultaneously when it is running short on inventory which means that the cycle time in ordering becomes shorter, more frequent with smaller lots. This type of situation helps both parties involved. It creates a continuous and steady flow of work for the supplier instead of having major highs and lows and retailers can depend on smaller inventory investments to satisfy the needs of its customers without stock outs.

Supply Chain Tradeoffs—EOQ Example

Interactive relationships among the various members of the supply chain mean that a decision by one member can directly and severely impact another member. In this chapter, we have discussed EOQ. The following example is an illustration of how to perform EOQ analysis and also shows how SCM decisions can impact various members of the supply chain.

The following formula is the basis of EOQ. It allows us to determine the point at which the *order quantity* creates a situation *where annual carrying costs and annual ordering costs are the same*. This EOQ is based on the premise that:

Total Cost of Inventory = Annual Carrying Cost + Annual Ordering Cost

This simple formula can be restated as

$$\text{Total Cost} = \frac{Q}{2}H + \frac{D}{Q}S$$

where Q is order quantity, $Q/2$ is average inventory on-hand, H is holding cost per unit, D/Q is number of orders per year, D is annual demand, and S is ordering cost per order.

The EOQ formula takes the Total Cost formula above and determines which quantity (Q) minimizes both the carrying and ordering costs. This is the point where holding costs and ordering costs are both minimized and are equal to one another.

EOQ Application Example

A local retiree who is a woodworker has contracted to manufacture a small wooden souvenir item for sale at the hospitality booth at the local visitors' center. The manager of that booth is agreeable to the woodworker delivering finished goods at the shop owner's convenience. The items are relatively small and lightweight, so the primary cost of shipping is the relatively fixed cost of a trip across town. Relevant data for the shop are as follows:

- Annual demand (D) = 3500 units
- Ordering (shipping) cost (S) = $12 per order (this ordering cost basically consists of loading the items into a 1956 GMC pickup truck and filling it up with gas for the round trip drive from the outskirts of town where the retiree lives)
- Holding cost (H) = $0.50 per unit per year (this cost is low because it consists of the retiree storing the souvenirs in the basement of his house)

At first, the manager of the hospitality booth doesn't care when the deliveries occur. Thus, the retiree decides to deliver the items in such a way as to reduce his total costs. Remembering his EOQ equations from his former job, he does the following:

- $$Q_{opt} = \sqrt{\frac{2DS}{H}} = \sqrt{\frac{2 \times 3500 \times 12}{0.5}} = 410$$

Thus, the retiree will wait until they have built 410 souvenirs then load of the truck and drive to the store. Now given this optimal Q, what are the retiree's total annual costs?

- The **ordering cost** is $\dfrac{DS}{Q} = \dfrac{3500 \times 12}{410} = \$102$

- The **holding cost** is $\dfrac{QH}{2} = \dfrac{410 \times 0.5}{2} = \$102.5$

- The **total cost** is $\dfrac{QH}{2} + \dfrac{DS}{Q} = 102 + 102.5 = \$204.50$

This continues for a while until the manager at the hospitality booth gets tired of receiving shipments at different times from all the vendors.

The manager then asks all the vendors to make deliveries once a month. Before agreeing, the retiree checks the costs of this new requirement.

First, the retiree must determine what the new Q is. Since $D/Q = 12$ (once a month) and demand has not changed, the retiree determines that the new Q is 292 instead of 410. Given that the following is true

- The **ordering cost** is $\dfrac{DS}{Q} = \dfrac{3500 \times 12}{292} = \$144$

- The **holding cost** is $\dfrac{QH}{2} = \dfrac{292 \times 0.5}{2} = \$72.92$

- The **total cost** is $\dfrac{QH}{2} + \dfrac{DS}{Q} = 144 + 72.92 = \$216.92$

The difference between this cost and the first optimal cost is $216.92 - $204.50 = 12.42, so the retiree decides to agree to the manager's request.

The manager of the hospitality booth has been taking MBA courses at Wright State University and learns about the wonders of JIT. The manager realizes that if all his suppliers made deliveries once a week then he wouldn't need the back room to store inventory. Instead, he could knock out the wall and nearly double his sales floor, possibly increasing sales. Or, he could not use the back room at all and sell it to someone else to reduce costs. Either way he comes out ahead. Thus, he tells all the suppliers to make deliveries once a week.

The retiree goes back and assesses the costs of once a week delivery. First, the retiree must determine what the new Q is. Since $D/Q = 52$ (once a week) and demand has not changed, the retiree determines that the new Q is now 67. Given that the following is true

- The **ordering cost** is $\dfrac{DS}{Q} = \dfrac{3500 \times 12}{67} = \$624$

- The **holding cost** is $\dfrac{QH}{2} = \dfrac{67 \times 0.5}{2} = \$16.83$

- The **total cost** is $\dfrac{QH}{2} + \dfrac{DS}{Q} = 624 + 16.83 = \$640.83$

The difference between these costs and the first (optimal) costs is $640.83 – $202.50 = $436.33. The retiree realizes that once a week delivery would eat up all the profit he is making. Since he is only doing this for fun, the retiree decides not to supply the hospitality booth any more but to devote his leisure time to fishing.

This particular EOQ example illustrates the issues involved with JIT. The entire concept of JIT has been heralded for years as a way for firms to reduce inventory and thus reduce costs. This allows firms to increase ROI and other financial measures. As a general rule, larger firms have embraced JIT concepts and asked their suppliers (usually smaller firms) to provide them with JIT deliveries. While large firms view JIT positively as a means to reduce costs, as a general rule, smaller firms have a different view of JIT. They refer to it as "I get to hold your inventory"—and the accompanying costs. Thus, supply chain managers need to understand that when implementing any new system (forecasting, planning and control, or distribution) they need to be aware of what the impact of that system will be to both upstream and downstream supply chain players. By incorporating those players in the initial planning and assessment, alternatives may be found. Even if no alternatives are found, at least the other members of the supply chain will know what is coming in plenty of time to adapt to the requisite changes.

Key Take-Aways

- Strong inventory management protects the company from overstocking, shortages, inaccurate logical information, and unsatisfactory ROI.
- The results of good inventory management include, but are not limited to, better forecasting, improved financial returns by reducing costs, identification of crucial products, and the ability to support JIT strategies.
- The tools of inventory management include EOQ modeling, Wagner–Whiten Procedure, MRP II, ERP, JIT, and ABC Classification. If you are not familiar with any of these, it would be beneficial to learn about those and run analyses to determine if they would be beneficial to your organization.

- Trends in inventory control include EDI, VMI, SBT, CPFR, and RFID. Keeping up to date on what is happening with these trends through trade organizations, customer contacts, and so forth, will give your company a competitive advantage. Even if you are not currently participating in these activities, you should be prepared to react in case you are asked to participate with any of your trading partners. Knowing the trends and your capabilities will allow you to respond quickly and decisively to such requests, gaining respect from your trading partners along the way.

Reflection Points

1. What are the main types of inventory control used in your company? How are they managed? What areas of inventory control have been the same for a long time? Numerous changes in best practices in recent years suggest that any processes that have not been evaluated, updated, or both, in the last 1–3 years are outdated.

2. Why has your firm adopted these inventory control methods? Was there an analysis of best methods or is it a case of "we've always done it this way"? Do your computer or electronic capabilities limit your options? Do you know what it would take to update your systems? Even if you don't plan to make changes it is prudent to know the alternatives and make a cognizant decision not to change, rather than to be complacent in a dynamic environment.

3. Has your company ever attempted to change inventory control methods? If so, how successful or unsuccessful was it? What were the key factors that led to that success or failure?

4. Do you or your team know how much your inventory control processes cost—holding costs, ordering costs, and so on? All processes should undergo a cost/benefit analysis on a regular basis. Additionally, understanding the cost of the processes as they pertain to different types of inventory is essential to help you make profitable inventory decisions.

5. Are you outsourcing any portion of your inventory control processes or requirements? Why or why not?

6. Are your customers pushing inventory control responsibilities upstream in the supply chain, in other words, pushing the responsibilities and carrying costs back to you? Do you know how this is affecting your company operationally and financially? Understanding these effects will allow you to negotiate from a stronger position when your customers make propositions like these in the future.

7. How would your customer respond to a request like Scan Based Trading? Do you have the financial capacity to carry the inventory of your customers?

Additional Resources

Chopra, S., & Peter, M. (2004). *Supply chain management: Strategy, planning and operation* (2nd ed.). Upper Saddle River, NJ: Pearson.

Donnan, S., & Peter, H. (1999). Designing a supply chain change process: A food distribution case. *International Journal of Retail & Distribution Management 27*(10), 409–420.

Olivia, R. & Noel, W. (2009, March/April). Managing functional biases in organizational forecasts: A case study of consensus forecasting in supply chain planning. *Production and Operations Management 18*(2), 138–151.

Ritzman, L. & Lee, K. (2003). *Foundations of operations management.* Upper Saddle River, NJ: Pearson.

Simchi-Levi, D. & Philip, K. (2003). *Designing and managing the supply chain concepts, strategies and case studies* (2nd ed.). Boston, MA: Irwin/Mcgraw-Hill.

Toomey, J. (2000). *Inventory management principles concepts and techniques.* Boston, MA: Kluwer Academic Publisher.

Worthen, B. (2003, January 15). Hot potato! *CIO Magazine.*

CHAPTER 6

Logistics

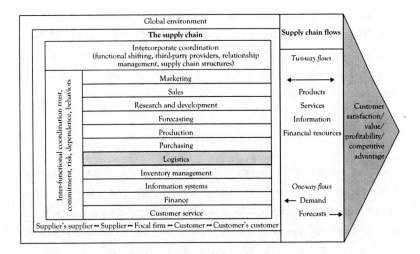

Chapter Objectives

- Introduce logistics within SCM
- Explore the transportation and delivery aspects of logistics
- Discuss cross-docking and its implications to business
- Share techniques about how to manage changes within a logistics system
- Examine the implications of international trade and distribution

Physical distribution has three primary concerns:

- **Receiving** raw materials, parts, packaging, or finished goods
- **Storing** these items until they are required, and
- **Delivering** them to the customer

The transfer of material from facility to facility, and ultimately to the customer, is the responsibility of the firm's distribution channel.

A bottleneck in this process can have detrimental consequences, such as increasing lead-time for completion of a product, raising costs and reducing margins, and can potentially lose a customer. This is a very important part of every business that should not be taken lightly. Remember that the sale will not take place without having the right goods in the **right place at the right time.**

Supply chain managers have to address several important distribution decisions. This includes that mode of transport to use, the physical architecture of your distribution system (including the number and location of distribution warehouses), and whether to own or contract-out warehousing and transport.

Transportation

There are many different types of transportation available to businesses. The most common are seen in the following figure. The figure also shows multimodal configurations. When two types or modes are combined, you have multimodal transport methods. For example, stocking trucks on a railcar for long distance shipping is called piggybacking.

Other methods do exist, but their application is minuscule in scope when compared to those shown in the figure. For example, in large urban areas bike couriers are sometimes practical due to the congestion of roads and proximity of customers. Even pipelines, which companies use for

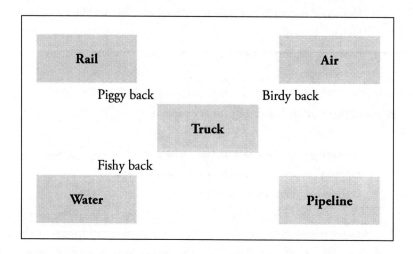

transportation of crude oil and natural gas from source to refineries, are limited in their availability. Thus, air, truck, rail, and water are the key transport methods used in most businesses.

Trucks have the advantage of being flexible. They also provide low loss and damage transport along with tracking, accuracy, and a wide geographical coverage. Another advantage is that there is currently heavy price competition in the trucking industry; thus, driving down costs. Unfortunately, weather and traffic conditions can delay truck shipments.

Railroads' advantages are that they provide inexpensive transport for carload size lots. However, this type of transportation requires that goods be packaged differently to allow for rough handling. While rail transport can be somewhat slow, the cost savings can be fairly substantial. Firms can also look to freight forwarders, piggybacking trucks, and double stacking containers for more opportunities for cost savings.

Water transport provides an alternative to air travel for overseas shipments for goods that are heavy, low value, and nonperishable. Containerization (the process of combining several unitized loads into a single well-protected load), strong port management, and port expansion increasing make water transport a reliable alternative. This form of transportation takes the most time, but is the best alternative when time is not of the essence.

Air transport is the transport method with the highest costs and smallest lead time. Thus, it is only suitable for high value, urgent, or perishable items. Weight and locations are limited; however, this type of transport saves on inventory holding costs because of the reduced transport times. This method is becoming more important in international trade.

In Europe, where the geography is more condensed and regulations permit high speed rail systems, rail is preferable to truck on both time and cost. In developing countries, the road infrastructure may be so poor that rail is again preferable to truck. Knowledge of the infrastructure in the area of operations is important to determine the best transportation methodology.

In addition, outsourcing should be considered for particular aspects in the distribution channel. While a company may have the equipment to transport materials from a manufacturing plant to the distribution center, it may not have the logistical capability to then deliver to its many customers. If it is international, then there might be a possibility that they lack the resources to effectively handle transportation in that country.

Delivery Methods

Once transportation decisions have been made, then delivery schedules must be set up. For most transportation modes there are two basic types of deliveries: direct and milk run.

Direct Deliveries

As the name implies, direct deliveries move goods from one origin facility to one receiving facility. Routing in this case is straightforward and usually consists of choosing the shortest direct path. Because of the direct nature of the transport, intermediary steps such as warehousing, shipment combination, and so forth are removed.

Milk Runs

As in some countries and many years ago in the United States, the milkman would deliver from a dairy store to multiple individual family homes. Hence, a **milk run** is a delivery system that delivers from a central origin to multiple locations. Milk runs are more complex than direct shipments. For example, decisions about quantities have to be made up front. Once this is determined, decisions must be made concerning the frequency of deliveries. Finally, scheduling must be done.

Delivery Techniques

Customer deliveries can be made from either single product locations or from distribution centers. Single product locations are ideal if you are dealing with high volumes of product with predictable demand. In that case the production facility or warehouse can deliver to customers in large bulk quantities thus allowing for large economies of scale.

Distribution centers (DCs) tend to be the primary facilities for most physical distribution structures because bulk quantities of different products must be combined in multiple ways and quantities to serve a large number of customers who may be located a great distance from the suppliers. DCs can warehouse inventory for future shipment or they can be used for cross-docking. This is a technique that was pioneered by Wal-Mart and has been embraced by many other firms.

Cross-Docking

When it comes to distribution techniques, cross-docking can be a strategic weapon in a successful physical distribution design, especially one that is heavily dependent upon execution and integration. Cross-docking can be viewed in several different ways. One might view it as combining both warehouse and distribution center functions. Another way of viewing it is as warehousing without inventory.

Cross-docks are essentially transshipment facilities to which trucks arrive with goods that must be sorted, consolidated with other products,

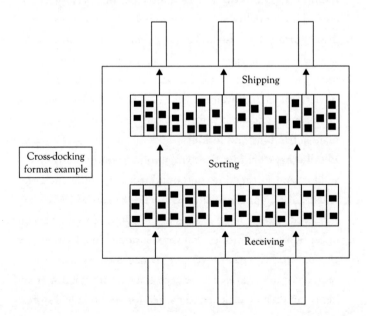

and loaded onto outbound trucks. Outbound trucks may be headed for a manufacturing site, a retail outlet, or another cross-dock, depending on the specific application.

The term *cross-docking* has been used to describe several different types of operations, all of which involve the rapid consolidation and shipment of products:

- **Manufacturing cross-docking:** Receiving and consolidating inbound supplies to support JIT manufacturing. For example, a manufacturer might lease a warehouse close to its plant in order to prepare subassemblies or consolidate kits of parts. Because demand for the parts is known, say from the output of an MRP system, there is no need to maintain stock.
- **Distributor cross-docking:** Consolidating inbound products from different vendors into a multi-SKU pallet, which is delivered as soon as the last product is received. For example, computer distributors often source components from different manufacturers and consolidate them into one shipment in merge-in-transit centers, before delivering them to the customer. An example may be a computer CPU, monitor, and keyboard are combined into one package at a cross-dock for delivery to the customer as a single package.
- **Transportation cross-docking:** Consolidating shipments from different shippers in the LTL and small package industries to gain economies of scale. For small package carriers, material movement in the cross-dock is by a network of conveyors and sorters; for LTL carriers it is mostly by manual handling and forklifts.
- **Retail cross-docking:** Receiving products from multiple vendors and sorting onto outbound trucks for different stores. Cross-docking has been cited as a major reason Wal-Mart surpassed K-Mart in retail sales in the 1980s. This is a version of centralized inventories that we mentioned in an earlier chapter. In this type of inventory management system, centralized inventories can be kept at a distribution center and items can then be picked and packed for an individual store

based on their needs. These are also called **Pick and Pack** or **Pick 'n Pack** systems. Many companies now utilize this type of system. There are sophisticated computer systems that assist in this process. One generic type is called "Pick to Light." This allows a warehouse employee to walk along a conveyor with a box and as they walk down the conveyor a light is turned on for each of the items that needs to be put into the box (the quantity is also indicated).

- **Opportunistic cross-docking:** In any warehouse, transferring an item directly from the receiving dock to the shipping dock to meet a known demand.

Ways to successfully implement cross-docking:

- Vendor cooperation
- Integrated information system with vendors
- High visibility and control
- Strong quality control program for the inbound
- Partnership with the vendors.

Advantages of cross-docking:

- Reduced handling costs
- Reduced inventory carrying costs
- Reduced cycle time/improved transit time
- Improved flexibility in opting for transportation mode
- Improved customer service
- Reduced space utilization.

Architecture

Depending upon the goals of the organization, there are many different types of ways that the supply chain's distribution system may be structured. If the firm is attempting to provide a high level of customer service with quick delivery times, then they may opt to have a decentralized hierarchy with many distribution centers scattered across the country. While this may incur additional costs, such as increased inventory and overhead from the additional facilities, it will almost ensure that they will be able to achieve their goals. If cost is the main driver, then a centralized warehouse and distribution network may be preferred, as this type of structure will allow for cost savings at the expense of delivery times.

Also, given the nature of the company's industry and products, the distribution system must be accommodating to factors of production. For industries that produce products with bulky raw materials that undergo a weight losing process (e.g., drilling, cutting, and stamping of raw iron into parts), manufacturing plants and distribution centers must be relatively close to the source of these inputs. Conversely, products that are subject to weight gaining activities (e.g., final assembly), where it is more economical to move the components than the final product, must be located toward the end of the supply chain near the consumer. Examples of these two concepts can be better explained by the steel industry and aerospace, where due to the bulk of iron ore, steel plants are located near the strip mines, and due to the size of jet fighters once finished, they are usually located near military facilities. A more extreme example of the latter would be the NASA program, where the space shuttle manufacturing facility is located approximately 3 miles away from the launch pad.

To summarize, when structuring your logistics and supply chain network, every structure is a variant of the extremes of centralized and decentralized. Both extremes have advantages. The key is to focus on the needs of your particular firm and its strategic position. Your distribution system's structure should follow from that.

Advantages of centralization include:

- Risk Pooling/Variance Reduction Effect
- Economies of Scale
- Economies of Scope
- Learning/Experience Curve
- Coordination Advantages

Advantages of decentralization include:

- Product/Process Improvements
  - Proximity to suppliers

- Customer Satisfaction
  - Proximity to markets/customers
- Cost Savings
  - Sourcing, Production, Logistics—Financing
- Risk Diversification/Portfolio Effect
  - Technology Risk—Financial Risk

Undergoing Distribution Changes

Steps for successfully altering an international supply chain's distribution system include:

- Conducting a comprehensive analysis of the infrastructure costs and customer service levels by channel, inventory levels, and product flow
- Developing a strategy to meet customer expectations, product availability, and delivery timing with lower operating costs
- Listing out the assumptions to be made at the planning stage
- Adopting a risk management approach early in the process
- Developing the target infrastructure to create a simpler and cost effective supply chain that was scalable
- Expecting the unexpected
- Having the right personnel at the right place
- Planning for change by balancing skills to unlock the complex combination of people and skills
- Developing a thorough organizational structure by balancing internal and external resources via:
  - steering group;
  - program management group;
  - business change group;
  - project management group;
  - project working group.

As simple as many of these principles are, many will recognize just how often the basics are ignored, thus burning through a large investment with no hope of a realistic return. The projects that are often considered **"too difficult"** or **"politically unacceptable"** might hold the secret to unlocking value. Before embarking on any major distribution restructuring, a supply chain manager should determine whether or not there is adequate support from senior management as well as all other levels in the organization; as such, a change will affect almost everyone in the company in one way or another.

Whatever the change in any business, remember

People are at the center of it

Things will go wrong that are not planned for

Things usually get worse before they get better and

You must maintain a sense of perspective through careful planning

---

Outsourcing in Distribution

As previously discussed, outsourcing is being used a great deal in SCM. One of the major areas of SCM outsourcing is distribution, specifically logistics.

Third Party Logistics (3PL)

There are many benefits to using third party logistics to handle many logistical functions that go beyond cost, such as more flexibility and increased customer satisfactions. It reduces the company's investments in vast logistic networks freeing capital and increasing flexibility. For example, Dell Computers has no internal delivery service, by outsourcing to UPS, they are able to deliver machines to their customers overnight at a lower cost than they could provide themselves. This frees Dell up to concentrate on their core business in lieu of a peripheral service such as delivery.

Fourth Party Logistics (4PL)

Fourth party logistics have evolved from of the outsourcing trend of third party service providers. 4PL relationships offer expanded services in comparison to 3PLs, which only deal with one aspect of the clients business (logistics). 4PLs often deal with inventory and vendor management, as well as distribution and logistics. The result can be better solution for the client, with more reliable service and results.

Freight Forwarding

When dealing with international shipments, there are several *extra* facets to transportation that must be attended to such as customs, duties, and so forth. This complicates the process and adds additional paperwork. As a result, many companies have outsourced international shipments to freight forwarders, that is, to companies that already have an expansive logistics capability, such as FedEx and DHL. In many cases these are turnkey types of relationships where the company turns over all of the responsibility for the freight until it clears customs in the destination country.

International Production and Distribution and SCM

There are many benefits to moving operations offshore. Free trade zones are attractive locations for companies to develop manufacturing facilities, where they are able to avoid duties and tariffs on the inputs of production that are not resold into the host county. Companies are able to exploit the lower labor costs and other incentives, and still are able to produce the product and ship it anywhere they desire.

Another reason for international expansion is proximity to emerging markets. Developing countries often provide a lucrative opportunity for firms that are willing to forgo initial profits to reap greater returns further down the line. In these cases, the firms employ a market share strategy and wager that once the country becomes rather affluent, they will have a sizable foothold in the country and recover their initial costs.

Expansion into foreign countries, however, often brings about new issues regarding the supply chain. Several of the constants that are taken for granted in the United States are not present in many other nations.

For example,

- Within the United States, the logistics capabilities are second to none. The existence of a vast highway system allows for freedom of movement to all parts of the country. These also extend into neighboring countries allowing for easy transportation by a single mode.
- In addition, there is an expansive rail network that allows for economical transportation of large quantities of goods to the major cities.
- Seaports have been built in all the major coastal cities, allowing for massive import/export operations and international trade.
- Airports are scattered across the nation, allowing overnight delivery to any part of the country. Some air service providers even offer deliveries within hours from one side of the country to the other, and to the major cities inbetween.
- Also, there is an elaborate telecommunication network that allows for the flow of information. Cellular, broadband, Wi-Fi, and satellite communications allow for companies to exchange and track information regarding their products.
- Computers are networked together so that people in different departments and even different cities can easily access information about a particular product.

Internationally, few nations have the capability discussed above, and as a result, companies must adapt to the differences in their host country. Many countries lack the infrastructure, making transportation difficult. Such is the case in China, where two-thirds of the roads are unusable for modern trucks. As a result, its chemical industry is suffering despite efforts of chemical manufacturers in China and the World Trade Organization. Additionally, utilities in many countries are not as sophisticated as those in the United States, and manufacturers may have to contend with rolling blackouts or brownouts. Infrastructure may not be as developed as well and firms must account for that variability in their transit times. For example, many countries do not have cellular service, and lack the advanced communications for computers. Some countries, such as Russia after the revolution, even had problems with basic telephone service.

In addition, the culture and political landscape may not be as hospitable in other countries as in the Unites States for US companies. In Japan, bribery is considered a part of business, and a necessity in order to remain competitive. This is in stark contrast to business practices in the United States, a plight that the US Olympic committee became all too familiar with after its bid for the winter games in Salt Lake City. Additionally, many Muslim countries have laws discriminating against women, so the company would be wise to take that into consideration before sending female expatriates overseas. Also, there might be some political instability that may affect the supply chain. Imagine a company losing a billion dollar facility to foreign nationals, such as the case of ChevronTexaco, who temporarily lost control of its refinery operations in Nigeria after unarmed village women stormed pipeline stations. Such an action would have a detrimental effect on the entire network, and ultimately to the company itself.

From a practical perspective, supply chain managers must accept the different aspects of managing inventory and distribution when the supply chain network moves from a domestic to a global structure. For example, higher inventories are given because of the longer lead times and increased uncertainty. The lead times are longer because distances are longer, transportation is more costly, and multiple modes are often required. As borders are crossed, delays are encountered, and new documentation is needed.

Multiple borders and countries also bring up the issues of managing physical distribution facilities and employees with different cultures, laws, and languages. A simple issue such as taking an order can be complex when the order-processing center is in a different country than the order and the languages involved are different. All these issues combine and service tends to be slower and more costly as buffer inventories are increased to keep service levels high.

Focus on Practice: European Methods of Integration

Europe has felt the effect of complex and overly complicated supply chain systems, which have historically required distribution centers in every country. These large, intricate systems have presented several problems for companies as they strive to stay competitive in the global marketplace. Several drivers are leading European companies toward integration of their physical distribution systems:

- Profit levels failing to meet management objectives
- Operational performance varying widely by brand, business, or unit
- Customer service levels not contributing to competitive differentiation
- Inventory levels high and rising higher with a poor demand–supply balance
- Suppliers and consumers not well linked to the overall company operations
- Companies in industries with rapid growth in the late 1990s
- Companies in traditionally low-growth sectors
- Companies with multiple brands running separate operations
- Multiple subsidiaries of multinational corporations.

Key Take-Aways

- Physical distribution has three primary concerns: receiving, storing, and delivering.
- Methods of transportation include, but are not limited to, rail, water, truck, air, and pipeline. Infrastructure in each country you plan to do business within is extremely important. You should know the transportation capabilities of countries in which you plan to distribute or manufacture.
- Cross-docking can be a key ingredient to satisfying your customers. Manufacturing, distributor, transportation, retail, and opportunistic cross-docking are different methods that you can use to satisfy your customers' or your own needs or requirements.
- Outsourcing distribution is a strategic option that should be undertaken only after engaging in a detailed analysis of how your company will benefit and what the costs will be to your organization and even your customers. Outsourcing in this arena can significantly benefit your business strategies if

administered correctly. Be certain to put processes in place to ensure the transparency of the 3PL or 4PL's activities and costs incurred on your behalf.

Reflection Points

1. What is the primary method of transportation that your firm uses in distribution? Why? How does this support your firm's competitive priorities?
2. Does your firm control its own distribution system or does it outsource it? Why or why not?
3. Is your distribution network centralized or decentralized? How do you think your network's structure relate to the answers you gave in questions 1 and 2?
4. Does your firm utilize cross-docking? Has it been pleased with the results? Have those results been measured?

Additional Resources

Begley, T. M., & Boyd, D. P. (2002, Winter). The need for a corporate global mind-set. *MIT Sloan Management Review* 25–32.

Bovet, B. (2004, January/February). Europe's new growth driver. *Supply Chain Management Review.*

Carsten, D., & Gruen, T. (2004, May). Stock-outs cause walkouts. *Harvard Business Review.*

Duris, R. (2003, September). The seven deadly sins of supply chain management. *Frontline Solutions.*

Eisenhardt, K. M. (2002, Winter). Has strategy changed. *MIT Sloan Management Review.*

MacMillan, I. C., van Putten, A. B., & McGrath, R. G. (2003, May). Global gamesmanship. *Harvard Business Review.*

Richardson, H. L. (2004, April 4). Execution at the dock. *Logistics Today.*

Schaer, B. (1997). Implementing a crossdocking operation. *IIE Solutions* 34–36.

Stalk, G., Evans, P., & Shulman, L. E. (1992). Competing on capabilities: The new rules of corporate strategy. *Harvard Business Review* 57–69.

New, S. (2010, October). The transparent supply chain. *Harvard Business Review* 88(10), 76–82.

Thomas, C., & Tom., L. (2011, December) Harvard Business Review. *Don't Let Your Supply Chain Control Your Business 89*(12), 112–117.

Zwolinski, K. (2003). Changing supplies. *Manufacturing Engineer* 14–17.

CHAPTER 7

Information Technology

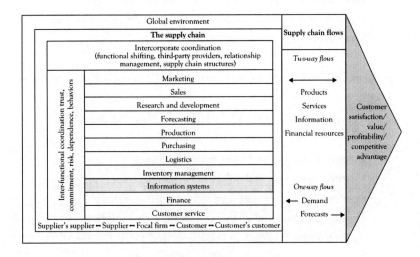

Chapter Objectives

- Introduce information technology (IT) as it exists today
- Explore the goals of IT in SCM
- Discuss different types of IT solutions in SCM
- Explore the advantages and difficulties associated with IT in SCM
- Consider trends and implementation issues in IT
- Apply IT issues through mini-cases

The business environment is changing and increasing the need for reducing uncertainty related to demand, supply, distance, and delivery time. This, coupled with an increasing need to closely manage activities, has necessitated the implementation of various information technologies (IT) to reduce uncertainty, improve coordination, and synchronization. To address these issues, several IT solutions have been created and are utilized at various levels of the supply chain. For example,

- **Upstream supply chain:** EDI, Extranets, Virtual Private Networks
- **Internal supply chain:** Intranets, Data Warehouse, ERP, MRP (I & II), traditional transaction processing systems, and Executive Information Systems.
- **Downstream supply chain:** Customer Relationship Management (CRM), Order Management System, and Web Services.

Key issues for the successful implementation of an IT-enabled SCM include:

- **Strategic planning for IT in SCM:** IT planning must have long-term vision to match the goals and objectives of SCM in terms of flexibility and responsiveness.
- **Virtual enterprise and collaborative commerce:** Establishing a network of firms to create a virtual organization. The advanced version of this concept is called CFPR (Collaborative Forecasting, Planning, and Replenishment).
- **Infrastructure:** Apart from the software and hardware, the training of personnel in the use of the technologies needs to be taken care of on a regular basis.
- **Creating and managing knowledge:** With vast reservoirs of information being generated, there is a tremendous opportunity to generate knowledge in order to be competitive in the marketplace.

What Is Information Technology (IT)?

Before we go further, it is important to clarify what we mean by information technology (IT). IT is an umbrella term that encompasses all forms of technology used to create, store, exchange, and use information in its various forms (business data, voice conversations, still images, motion pictures, multimedia presentations, and other forms, including those not yet conceived). It's a convenient term for including both telephony and computer technology in the same word. It is the technology that is driving what has often been called "the information revolution"—whatis.com.

The information revolution has been considered the next revolution after the "railroad revolution" or the transport revolution that linked the whole country. IT has also impacted the management of supply chain. The question then arises, "what are the key issues in supply chain management that IT can help to address?"

Goals of Supply Chain Information Technology

The primary goal of IT in the supply chain is to link the point of production with the point of delivery or purchase. This allows planning, tracking, and estimating lead times based on real data. To utilize information, we need to collect it, access it, analyze, and have the ability to share it for collaboration purposes. In this sense, supply chain system goals are:

- **Collecting information:** Every company in the supply chain needs to know the status of its information. For this reason, it is important that the information be accessible by the various locations within a company. Information needs to be collected and then stored in such a way that it is accessible by multiple users, in various distributed locations. Adding to the complexity of collecting and storing information is the fact that the participants need to see data in different terms, manners, and measurements.
- **Access to data:** The goal here is that all the available information can be accessed, regardless of the mode of inquiry used (e.g., phone, fax, etc.) or who is making the inquiry. Ideally, everyone who needs to use certain data should have access to the same real-time data through any interface device as represented in the following figure (e.g., with banking applications you can access the same account from almost everywhere).
- **Analysis based on supply chain data:** The information must be analyzed and utilized to find the most efficient ways to produce, assemble, warehouse, and distribute products. To facilitate this, an IT system must be flexible enough to accommodate changes in supply chain strategies.

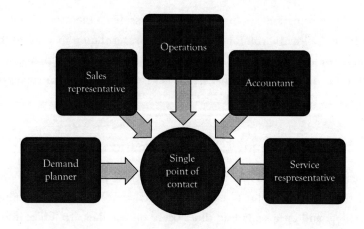

- **Collaboration with supply chain partners:** Success depends on the ability to collaborate with partners. This requires not only sophisticated alignment of IT systems but also the integration of business processes. IT collaboration has led to the event of two systems: supplier relationship management (SRM), the ability to link and work effectively with suppliers, and customer relationship management (CRM), to provide better contact and understanding customer needs.

IT Solutions for SCM

IT is primarily used for managing flow of information across an organization's supply chain. IT is also employed for efficient storage and retrieval of the information. Different technologies are used with different portions of the supply chain. Thus, we need to view various technologies from the perspective of where they fit in the supply chain.

The Upstream Supply Chain

Based on your role in the supply chain, the upstream part may consist of suppliers, manufacturers, or distributors. All the entities in the supply chain from which you are procuring the goods or services form the upstream part of supply chain. Some of the technologies that are widely used with this portion of supply chain are:

- **EDI:** Electronic Data Interchange (EDI) is commonly defined as computer-to-computer electronic exchange of business documents in a standard format. The benefits of using EDI include:
  - Reduced costs for order processing
  - Improved communication
  - Electronic verification, automation, and less error-prone.
- **E-Business:** E-Business is business primarily conducted over various networks using web technology to streamline business processes. The benefits of E-business include:
  - Increased productivity and efficiency
  - Trusted and easy communication with vendors, partners, and customers
  - Redefines traditional business models to maximize customer experience. E-commerce is facet of E-business.
- **Extranets:** Extranets connect several Intranets via Internet by adding to the Internet security mechanism. They form some kind of virtual network between organizations. The benefits of extranets in SCM are:
  - Reduction of cooperation and operational costs
  - Expedite and secure information delivery
- **Internet with client/server scheme:** Client–server schemes are used in Internet commerce to provide an extra layer of security. The primary benefit of this approach is enhanced and increased connectivity options offered to agents external to a supply chain.

The Internal Supply Chain

The internal part of the supply chain includes all the inhouse processes used in transforming the inputs received. The internal supply chain is mainly concerned with production management, manufacturing, and inventory control. The ways IT is used with internal supply chain are:

- **Intranets:** An Intranet is the use of web to create a private network of the organization. Some benefits of Intranets are:
  - Increased availability of company information to trusted users
  - Increased security by using firewalls or other safety mechanisms

- **Data warehouses:** Proper storage and management of data is very critical. Data warehouses provide storage of data in different formats that are widely used. The advantage of using data warehouses is you can get all the information you want from one place. Access to the data in warehouse is transparent to user irrespective of its storage location.
- **ERP systems:** An ERP information system integrates all the applications related to internal supply chain. Some benefits of using ERP software are:
  - Force business process reengineering (BPR): BPR is an approach that aims at improving business tasks to achieve organization's goals
  - Reduction of cost
  - Multiple functionalities like data storage, transaction processing, planning, and so forth may be provided as part of ERP software
- **Transaction processing software:** The IT system in which the computer responds immediately to user requests. The benefits of using transaction processing software are:
  - Reduced overhead
  - Faster response to customer demands and thus improves customer experience
- **Executive information systems (EIS):** EIS is a set of forecasting and planning tools to assist senior management. The benefits of using EIS are:
  - Improved strategic planning
  - Executive Decision making support
  - Expedite business decisions

The Downstream Supply Chain

The downstream supply chain includes all the activities in delivering the final products to customers who may be other organizations. Some of the emerging technology trends that are used include:

- **Web services:** Web services provide service to customers or other businesses. These are self-contained, self-describing modules aimed at application integration. Advantages of using web-services include:
  - Increased availability
  - Easy to extend
  - Increased interoperability with other systems
- **Order management software:** System that receives customer order information and inventory availability from warehouse management system and then processes the orders. The benefits of using this technology are:
  - determines the inventory levels and trigger actions automatically;
  - groups the customer order according to priority and requirements; and
  - establishes order delivery dates and notifies customers.
- **CRM software:** CRM systems are used to keep track of company's most valuable assets—their customers. The benefits of using CRM software are:
  - creates properly managed information about customers;
  - analysis and mining tools for extracting customer information; and
  - automate the process and reduces paper overhead.

Advantages and Difficulties of IT

Time Management

Using an IT system that can measure several aspects of how much time is being used for processes and other business functions can aid a company in analyzing where time is being wasted, identify any bottle necks in a process, and can show where time is best being utilized. This will help with scheduling manpower, purchasing, and manufacturing to make organizations more efficient or productive by shortening the amount of time it takes to complete a given amount of work.

Improved Customer Experience

Customer Experience Management (CEM), an IT tool, immediately generates reports and analyses. Managers use this information to proactively respond to customer service and satisfaction issues. From the voice of the customer and integrating customer-generated information into the research and development cycle, companies reduce the risk of developing products not required by the market place. Using CEM as an IT tool demonstrates the power of collecting relevant customer information, developing and implementing winning strategies, and measuring their results.

Social and Cultural Issues and Resistance

Users are reluctant to invest time to learn a new tool if they already know ways to perform tasks using culturally proven, familiar technology. IT, particularly the computer, is not culturally neutral. It often reflects the nature of the country in which it was developed or manufactured. One of the most distinct problems of developing countries in fostering IT is their cultural difference from Western societies where individualism and rationalism are accepted as the higher values of life. Some jobs require retraining, others, many of them unskilled, would disappear or would be replaced with a cheaper alternative to personnel. Thus, the question of introducing IT in countries where the unemployment rate is increasing each year becomes an important consideration.

Expatriation

In a global economy, gathering information and using IT tools in different countries can be difficult. It is best to go into a country knowing the culture so that the right information can be gathered and proper factors taken into account during analyses. Expatriation issues are a growing problem for many international firms. From an SCM perspective, the organization determines the importance of international operations and the nature of international assignment. It then develops activities that are necessary to prepare personnel for foreign assignment.

Important Developments for a Successful IT-Enabled SCM

Companies are now trying to improve their ability to be flexible and responsive in an electronically connected and dynamic world to meet the changing market. Companies need to intensify their efforts in developing information and communication technologies to overcome the complexity of the buyer–supplier system. In this regard, some critical areas for the successful development of an IT-enabled SCM are discussed in this section.

Strategic Planning for IT in SCM

Almost all companies are now focusing on strategic planning with the objective of developing long-term plans and making changes to their organizations in order to improve their competitiveness. Strategic planning of IT should support the long-term objectives and goals of SCM, both in terms of flexibility and responsiveness to changing market requirements.

For example, IT can facilitate rapid partnership formation by making the right information available and developing a virtual enterprise. Some important issues to be considered in strategic planning are:

- **Marketing IT in SCM:** Companies need to reconfigure their resources to compete in a new market and meet changing requirements. This requires organizations to have an effective supply chain or a physically distributed enterprise.
- **Economic reasons:** Factors such as customer requirements, competitors, and price force organizations to change the way they manage their operations. Unsurprisingly, flexibility and responsiveness are all directly associated with cost.
- **Organizational reasons:** Strategic planning of IT in SCM includes organizational issues such as structure, awareness of management, business processes, and strategic alliances. All of these items are factors that influence the overall performance of an IT-enabled SCM.
- **Technological reasons:** Strategic planning involves decisions that affect the long-term performance of an organization. For example, lack of IT in an organization can make it obsolete because it cannot qualify as a partner in a virtual enterprise.

Virtual Enterprise in SCM

Virtual enterprise or virtual organization is based on developing a network of collaborative firms with necessary core competencies for reaching the market on time with the right product. To develop such a network, companies require a communication system that supports its goals. This can be achieved by utilizing various telecommunication technologies. Some important issues to be considered in virtual enterprises are:

- **Partnership:** It is necessary that a partnership be open to innovation and trust due to growing networks and services delivered through the Internet.
- **Virtual teams and supply chain:** Virtual teaming is the most appropriate mechanism to examine the relationship between all parties along the value chain.
- **Virtual enterprise and IT:** Virtual enterprise is based on similar strategies. Distance across the partners, however, may create communication problems later.

E-commerce

E-commerce can take a variety of forms such as EDI, Internet, Intranet, extranet, E-mail, and others. The necessity of communication and coordination is required to support the interorganizational sharing of resources and competencies. Some important issues to be considered in E-commerce are:

- **Purchasing:** Purchasing practice has multiplied tremendously since the increased popularity of E-commerce. Examples of this benefit are cost savings resulting from reduced paper transactions, shorter order-cycle time, inventory reduction, and enhanced opportunities for supplier/buyer partnership through communication networks.
- **Operations:** The adoption of more integrated I-commerce models should strengthen the relationship between a network orientation and a global SCM. The Internet makes foreign

markets more accessible and makes it easier to integrate overseas customers, suppliers, and intermediaries into a closely managed supply chain relationship.

Infrastructure for IT in SCM

Infrastructure for IT in SCM consists of Internet connectivity, hardware, and software including application system integration. Training and education for IT is important to understand so that the full technology can be utilized. There are different IT platforms and systems available to enable the application of IT in SCM. Some important issues to be considered in infrastructure are:

- **Organizational:** Adoption of E-business involves deep level changes that affect core elements of an organization, including mission, vision, business strategy, goals, culture, technology, training, and policies.
- **Technological:** Technological innovations, such as advances in ERP systems, have come in abundance in the past decade which has played a major role in developing SCM. Also, developments in hardware and telecommunication technologies have occurred in order to meet the rising demand.

Knowledge and IT Management in SCM

Knowledge management is concerned with recognizing and managing all organization's assets to meet its business objectives. Organizations have redesigned their internal and external structure, creating a knowledge network to facilitate improved data communication, while improving coordination, decision making, and planning. Some important issues to be considered in knowledge and IT management are:

- **Technology management:** Information technology such as XML for representing corporate data, ERP infrastructure that provide support for logistics operations, and web infrastructure allow B2B E-commerce to be successful for SCM. In the emerging E-procurement marketplaces, firms establish efficient web-based electronic relationships that allow for closer integration between buyer and supplier.

- **Educating and training:** Educating and training are the most important components of any change in an organization. In order to be successful, companies need to have full cooperation of employee at all levels; otherwise, technologies alone will not help to improve the organizational competitiveness.

Implementation of IT in SCM

People and processes in an organization must be adaptable in order to respond successfully to the introduction of new IT processes and systems. The changes are often drastic and cause organizational tension. Integration of supply chain activities and processes that were in place prior to IT systems development and implementation in the supply chain is helpful for a successful and uneventful implementation and transition.

- **Organizational:** Top management support is a fundamental requisite for a successful implementation of IT. Also, the nature of the employee skill and experience with IT systems and transitions also influence the success of implementation.
- **Methodological:** Methodological issues of IT implementation in SCM are important, as well. Some companies choose to reengineer their business processes with the objective of implementing IT and improving their performance. Implementation teams should be cross-functional and able to address methodological issues as they arise.
- **Cultural (human resources):** Behavioral attitude toward the implementation of IT in SCM, level of education, knowledge in computers, international exposure, training and education, reward and employee empowerment, and incentive schemes also impact the successful implementation of IT in SCM. These items should be considered while designing systems and planning their implementation.

Mini-Case Examples of IT Usage

An IT application is very important to a business' supply chain. The application needs to be able to gather needed data, store the data, and then retrieve the data so that it can be used in a meaningful and correct way. Some companies have been able to use and apply their IT systems so that they gain the upper hand with respect to their competition. Some examples follow.

Mini-Case: Dell and Wal-Mart Stores

These two companies devastated their competition by reinventing their supply chains and are now firmly established as dominant players in their business. IT and SCM were key components of their continued success.

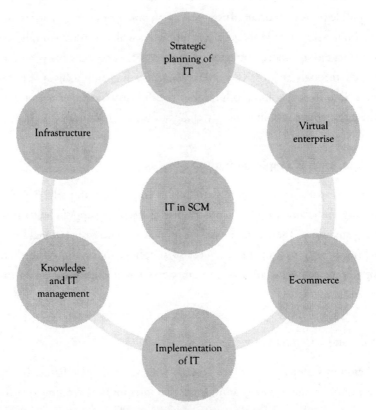

Framework for development of IT for effective SCM

Wal-Mart uses a huge IT network to let suppliers know what and when products are needed. They are constantly in the forefront of new technologies trying to implement what they believe will support their strategic focus of low-cost operations. Dell_uses the Internet to manage ordering information. A customer puts in their order and the system assigns a barcode to the job. All the information on the product, from when it was built, how long it took at different processes, to when it was shipped is stored in Dell's IT network and has helped with all types of forecasting.

Such IT applications use a mix of design and planning and may include modules for managing demand, distribution, production, material requirements, purchasing, and fulfillment. Some supply chain applications include multimodule systems for managing warehousing, transportation, customer relationships, and supplier relationships. There are also newer systems for monitoring the chain as a whole and responding to problems as they occur. These packages come from many vendors and are built using a wide range of technologies, which further complicates the integration process. Integration problems are gradually being solved, largely through major ERP vendors incorporating supply chain applications into their flagship products, but the industry hasn't yet matured to the point where installing supply chain software is reliable.

Mini-Cases: Examples of Failure

What happens when an IT system fails or is not used properly? The following are examples of the importance of keeping supply chains running smoothly. These companies lost money, but these operational losses represent only part of the true cost of supply chain failures. The more significant problems arise when companies reveal their mistakes to the financial markets.

Nike and Cisco Systems

These two companies ran into trouble with their supply chains. In the case of Nike, the company announced that sales for the preceding quarter were $100 million lower than expected because of confusion in its supply chain caused by a failed installation of i2 Technologies Inc.'s APS system. This loss was eclipsed by Cisco's announcement that it was writing down $2.2 billion in unusable inventory due to problems in its supply chain. The writedown was, in large part, due to a materials planning system that allowed demand for components to be double and triple counted across its suppliers.

Kmart Corp.

The Company announced in May 2000 that it was spending $1.4 billion on software and services to overhaul its supply chain, including planning systems and warehouse management software. A year and a half later, before the system went live, Kmart announced that it was abandoning most of the software it had purchased and was instead buying $600 million worth of warehouse management software from Atlanta-based Manhattan Associates Inc. This new push also failed to solve the company's supply chain problems, and it went into bankruptcy in January 2002.

What can be learned from these failures? The industry needs to support yet another generation of enterprise applications, with all the growing pains and integration problems. Although supply chain management software forms a tidy category, it is an odd assortment of packages from a variety of vendors, which makes integration more complicated and information harder to obtain.

Key Take-Aways

- Integrating Information Technology into your company is a grand idea. It can add tremendous value to the company and make the supply chain more efficient. However, there are some concerns that will need to be addressed. Most of the IT used in supply chain comes under the banner of "interorganizational systems (IOS)" and there are many important factors that impact the success/failure of IOS.
  - **Partners:** A collaboration that is willing to cooperate and work together is vital. There must be willing participants that are involved so that information sharing is possible

even when the entities have different objectives and different partners.

- **Common technological standards**: IT is strictly dependent on technology, integration, and data access. It is imperative that all companies keep up with industry standards so that all the information that is gathered can be accessed and used to help the supply chain run efficiently. This includes keeping up with emerging technology and taking the risk to changes ones core business processes when methodologically necessary.
- **Education and training:** New technologies that are available must be taught to those people who will use the technology, so that the program is not underutilized. Again it is important to emphasize that the employees will need to be educated and trained with regard to the IT systems and the underlying methodological processes that will need to be changed. If the employees do not understand why things are changing, they are unlikely to conform and, in our experience, will work around the system to maintain the status quo.
- **Cross-cultural issues:** With the global economy, it is important to understand cultural differences so that they can be taken into account when data is captured and analyzed.
- **Resistance to change:** With many new emerging technologies, a company must be willing to adapt and change strategies when it is necessary.
- Variations of IT support for supply chain functions include:
  - **Upstream supply chain:** EDI, E-Business, extranet, Internet with client/server scheme.
  - **Internal supply chain:** Intranets, data warehouses, ERP, transaction processing software, and executive information systems.
  - **Downstream supply chain:** Web services, order management software, and CRM software.

Reflection Points

1. How well do your IT systems support the goals of your supply chain? Do they support the integration and coordination of internal and external participants in your value chain? Which of the IT strategies listed above does your company not utilize and why?

2. Have you ever thought of your IT system as it specifically supports your supply chain? Does your IT system have modules implemented that support the various aspects of the supply chain?

3. Are there any processes in your organization that needed to be changed when IT systems were implemented, but were never truly updated? How would you know if work -arounds have been put into place in order to maintain the status quo?

Additional Resources

Bal, T., & Teo, P. K. (2000). Implementing virtual teamworking. Part 1: A literature review of best practice. *Logistics Information Management 13*(6), 346–352.

Chopra, S., & Meindl, P. (2004). *Supply chain management: Strategy, planning and operation* (2nd ed.). Upper Saddle River, NJ: Pearson.

Grossman, M. (2004). The role of trust and collaboration in the internet-enabled supply chain. *Journal of American Academy of Business 51*, 391–396.

Gunasekaran, A. (2003). *Information systems in supply chain integration and management.* The Netherlands: Elsevier.

Hewitt, F. (2001). After supply chains, think demand pipelines. *Supply Chain Management Review.*

Kumar, K. (2001). Technology for supporting supply chain management. *Communications of the ACM 44*(6), 58–61.

Lee, H. (2002). Aligning supply chain strategies with product uncertainties. *California Management Review 44*(3), 105–119.

Lee, H. (2010, October). Don't tweak your supply chain—Rethink it end to end. *Harvard Business Review 88*(10), 62–69.

Lei, D. & Slocum, J. (1992). Global strategy, competence-building and strategic alliances. *California Management Review.*

Simchi, D. & Kaminsky, P. (2003). *Designing & managing the supply chain concepts, strategies & case studies* (2nd ed.). Boston, MA: McGraw-Hill/ Irwin

Turban, E., & Wetherbe, J. (2004). *Information technology for management* (4th ed.). New York: John Wiley & Sons.

Varner, I., & Palmer, T. (2002). Successful expatriation and organizational strategies. *Review of Business 23*(2), 8–11.

Website Reference

http://www.viradix.com/terminology.html

CHAPTER 8

Customer Service

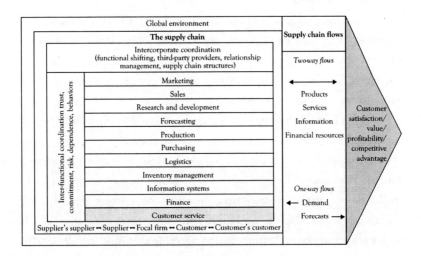

Chapter Objectives

- Introduce customer service as an SCM concept
- Discuss customer satisfaction
- Explore service quality
- Consider how to measure and manage performance
- Examine the balanced score card concept

William Davidow and Bro Uttal in their book, *Total Customer Service*, state that "the war of business has shifted onto a new battle ground… The spoils will go to those few companies that both perceive the need for outstanding service and take the steps necessary to delivery it." Many companies have embraced the idea that they need to focus on customer service. What they have neglected are the actions necessary to actually deliver it.

In order to deliver exceptional customer service through the supply chain we need to view it in the context of a service supply chain. For example, Figure 8.1 outlines what supply chain managers should focus upon in order to provide not only customer service, but also customer satisfaction. The total service quality management process is the summation of focusing on the various elements of the cultural, social, and legal environment while aggressively managing your human resource and supply chain operations.

The strategic context is stooped in the cultural, social, and legal environment. With data on customer expectations within different environments and situations, a company will know what to do in order to keep customers satisfied, and will have the necessary information to set successful objectives and service standards.

Supply chain operations have a greater influence in the second step—building the organization. It is in this step that the service delivery system is designed, and a sound supply chain is the foundation of the delivery system. The importance of human resources can be seen in the majority of the service quality management process steps. Human resources are responsible for developing capabilities and managing performance, which includes measuring, evaluating, and recognizing performance, along with rewarding high performers. Hence, this conceptual framework can be used to manage high service quality in any industry. This chapter will outline some of the key concepts in this process.

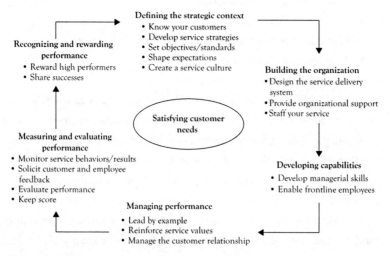

Figure 8.1. The service quality management process.

Customer Service as a Supply Chain Concept

Today, many companies have a customer service standard, which is a statement of goals and acceptable performance for the quality of service that a company expects to deliver to its customers. This is all well and good, but what many companies fail to realize is that service operations (which encompasses all aspects of customer service) is a supply chain concept. Specifically, the customer experience is a chain of contacts the customer undergoes in obtaining a product as shown in Figure 8.2. Each link represents a contact. Just as in SCM, the total experience depends on the weakest link.

Thus, the customer experience includes any episode in which the customer comes in contact with the organization. This includes contacts via person, phone call, mailing, advertising, and Internet interactions, just to name a few. Thus, any event that forms a perception of the organization in the mind of the customer (both positively and negatively) can impact potential sales. That is why service operations are so important to SCM. Let's take a moment for a quick mini-case to emphasize this point.

Mini-Case Study: Caterpillar Corp.

Caterpillar is the world's leading manufacturer of construction and mining equipment, diesel and natural gas engines, and industrial turbines. One of Caterpillar's key SCM strengths is its ability to provide over 620,000 discrete service parts to keep customers up and running even when they are literally around the globe. Former Caterpillar Chairman Don Fites often referred to product support as the "corporate jewels." The reason for that is that Caterpillar customers rate product support as the number one factor in generating repeat business.

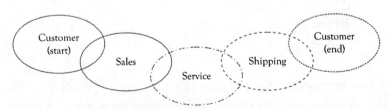

Figure 8.2. Customer service—A supply chain concept.

This capability is not taken for granted; during the last 15 years, Caterpillar has continually improved its service parts supply chain. That improvement has been measured by reducing inventory by more than half while improving on customer service levels that were already the envy of the industry. Their customer service supply chain performance can be measured in various ways. For example, over 99% of the time Caterpillar can ship an order in less than 24 hours. This would be impossible to accomplish without an efficient supply chain, and Caterpillar's supply chain productivity has increased by more than 60% during that time. All these metrics reflect particular operational issues, but all of them combine into savings. For Caterpillar, their improvements have saved the company more than $460 million annually—while continuing their outstanding customer service.

Customer Service by Understanding the Environment and Customer

Service operations consist of all company operations that are not purely manufacturing. Services can be broadly divided in two groups, those that are purely services and those that are associated with the manufacturing sector. In the purely service sector they can be further divided into public and private. Examples include:

- In the Public sector:
  a) Health
  b) Social services
  c) Local authority services (i.e., schools, recreation, parks).
- In the Private sector:
  a) Cleaning
  b) Laundry
  c) Hotels and restaurants
  d) Banking
  e) Insurance.

Service operations in the manufacturing sector are supporting functions such as transport and distribution, office services, maintenance, customer support, and so forth. As products across industries become commodities, superior service is often left as the last true differentiator between companies. Being customer-centric, therefore, is no longer a "nice-to-have" ideal, but a necessary ingredient for success.

Knowing the Customer and Customer Retention

In moving toward a more customer-centric service model, a company must know how to approach customer service. Building stronger and more profitable customer relationships is crucial in today's global market. This is a powerful competitive weapon that companies have available in order to retain customers; however, there is not a specific recipe for building such relationships. As customers differ from place to place, and business to business, the strategies needed to build strong customer relationships vary accordingly. For this reason, knowing who your customers are and what their expectations are (even when they are changing) becomes essential. There are 10 common expectations that management should keep in mind.

1. Be accessible
2. Treat customers with courtesy
3. Be responsive to customers' needs and wants
4. Do what you are asked to
5. Provide well-trained and informed employees
6. Tell customers what they should expect from you
7. Meet your commitments and keep your promises
8. Do it right the first time
9. Follow up
10. Be socially responsible and ethical

The fact that not all customers are the same holds an opportunity for companies rather than a constraint. When companies handle customers differently based on needs and expectations, the value of each customer relationship, which is based on customer segmentation, will be optimized. Companies not only need to understand customer needs, but they also need to anticipate those needs whenever possible. Only then companies will be able to make the right offer to the right person at the right time.

In order to deliver quality service to customers, companies need to continually enhance customer experiences in the competitive marketplace. Evidence indicates that satisfying customers, however, is not sufficient to retain them. In fact, what determines the loyalty or defection of a customer depends on how delighted or outraged a customer is with the company's behavior. Thus, focusing on customer delight and outrage may lead to a better understanding of the dynamics of customer emotions and their effect on consumer behavior and loyalty. On the one hand, when customer needs are gratified with reliability, responsiveness, and assurance, they will be delighted. On the other hand, when customers' needs or desires are violated, they will be outraged.

The economics of attracting and retaining customers underscores the reason behind placing customers—not products—at the center of operations. Research consistently shows that it is five to seven times more expensive to find a new customer than to retain an existing one; however, it is prudent to remember that only valuable customers are worth retaining. All too often, in our experience, unprofitable customers are retained at detrimental expense to the company. Customer relationships must be aggressively managed, and those that are unprofitable, detrimental, or both, to the company should be severed. But, it does not mean that you should mistreat "low value" customers since you have an image and reputation to maintain in a specific industry. This simply means that the company should be keenly aware of its profitability by customer and understand the impacts of each customer's needs and desires on the company as a whole so that well-informed decisions can be made with regard to customer retention.

Customer Satisfaction

Generally speaking, high customer satisfaction can generate repurchase intentions, favorable word-of-mouth, and loyalty. There are three main components of customer satisfaction: price, product quality, and service quality. These are the components that a company can control. Situational and personal factors will also affect overall customer satisfaction, but these cannot be controlled, see Figure 8.3.

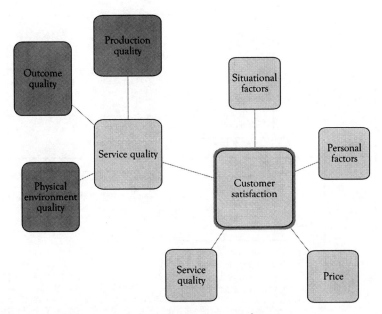

Figure 8.3. Factors impacting customer satisfaction.

For a company to be customer- or demand-driven, it must know who needs what, and when they need it. This information must be available across the organization with as much lead time as possible, so that managers can create and assign the most efficient schedules and routes for delivery as possible. By obtaining a better understanding of demand, the company can improve the economics of each delivery while still ensuring customer satisfaction. All the above elements determine how consumers perceive a company's service quality. In an attempt to establish a competitive advantage, marketing practitioners often seek to differentiate their offering upon service quality in order to ensure customer satisfaction.

A Gaps Model of Service Quality was developed in the late 1980s. This model shows five gaps that can affect, either positively or negatively, service quality and customer satisfaction. If each element of this model is well understood, managers can easily recognize where they hold weaknesses and make the required modifications to increase customer satisfaction (Figure 8.4). The five gaps fall between:

- what customers expect and what managers perceive they expect (Gap 1);

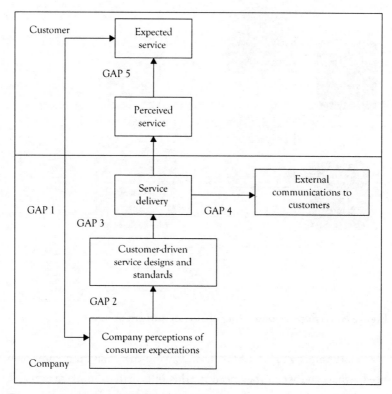

Figure 8.4. Gaps model of service quality.

- managers' perceptions of customers' expectations and the actual specifications they establish for service delivery (Gap 2);
- service specifications and the actual service delivered (Gap 3);
- what a company promises about a service and what it actually delivers (Gap 4);
- expected and perceived service from the customers' standpoint (Gap 5, the net effect of the last 4 gaps).

Service Quality: Building the Organization and Developing Capabilities

Service quality is an important precursor of customer assessment of values. It will in turn influence customer satisfaction and motivate behavioral intentions. In other words, the way a company manages its service operations reflects on how customers perceive the service quality. In order to establish competitive advantage, marketers often seek to differentiate their service offering upon service quality. There are both external and internal factors that will influence service quality. Social and legal environments, along with culture, are the external factors the company should understand and be prepared to react to accordingly. With respect to the internal factors, human resources and the supply chain, the company has to manage them in such a way as to meet the maximum number of customers' needs and desires in order to ensure high quality service.

Culture

Culture is an accumulation of learned meaning within a human population. These learned meanings or values provide guidance in their behavior as consumers. Recent research suggests that culture plays a fundamental role in determining how consumers perceive what constitutes service quality. Different cultures provide consumers with rules that guide their evaluation of service quality simply because what is feasible in a country might not be feasible in another country. Since it is challenging to integrate individuals of diverse backgrounds into a coherent organization, one has to be culture sensitive in order to deal with conflicts that emerge as a result of cultural differences. Transferring new procedures and concepts to members of another culture are more difficult than imagined. Also, learning to operate within a new culture involves questioning and articulating previously taken-for-granted beliefs and assumptions.

Knowledge of the local culture is important in order to recognize differences in consumer behavior. Even if the company is successful in managing cultural conflicts within the organization, it faces yet another challenge in order to understand local customers. They may have particular needs, expectations, and service quality perceptions with which the company has no experience. Redesigning operations may be necessary to meet and exceed those new expectations to ensure a high quality service perception. That is why standardization is not always possible and a degree of flexibility is highly desirable. For instance, McDonald's had to completely forgo its "beef specialty" and instead offer lamb and veggie patties in India.

Social and Legal Environments

Global markets mean that there are many countries offering immense opportunities for international companies, but their success often hinges on how they adapt their operations to the diverse social and legal environments in different localities. Even though these factors are external to the company, they often have huge influence on many areas of the company's operations. As an illustration, McDonald's, an active proponent of diversity, offers separate dining sections for men and women in Saudi Arabia to suit the local social environment. Pizza Hut's Moscow facility presents one of the examples of issues to be addressed in a foreign legal environment. Due to local laws, Pizza Hut had agreed to transfer management of the joint venture over to Russians eventually. Therefore, whether the Russian managers would be able to take over operations and maintain a high service quality became a major concern.

Human Resources Management

An organization that knows how to grow globally translates its winning people and employment practices into many different cultural settings. This cultural sensitivity spills over to the company's HR practices. Many successful companies employ positive and customer-service oriented people while ensuring that all the employment practices, policies, and regulations are met. As the company moves through its selection process, it looks at specific skill, general knowledge, customer service abilities, and experience in potential employees. Since finding, developing, and retaining the best people is one of the most important functions in HR, it can be seen as an integral part of the success of a company. As it was stated in McDonald's 1994 annual report, "In a copycat world, the best way to stand out from the crowd is through customer satisfaction—100% of the customers, 100% of the time ... It's no longer enough to measure restaurant performance by our internal standards, no matter how exacting. Success has to be measured through the eyes of the customer and the people who serve them."

Therefore, HR is a crucial factor to service operations. Its value can be seen as hiring, training, developing managerial skills, appraising, rewarding, and retaining the right managers and employees. The people who interact with customers should be carefully selected and trained to be able to deal with unexpected situations. Many times, it is not the problem that makes the customer dissatisfied but the inability of employees to promptly react to that situation. Proper training can prepare employees better for such situations, but it is also a matter of selecting people with the right attitude and giving them some degree of autonomy to make decisions themselves. As a motivation to maintain high performance levels, performance has to be constantly evaluated and high performers rewarded. Also, the role of the employees "behind the counter" should not be underestimated. Often, the last touch point of customer service is the only one that the customer evaluates for total service quality and overall customer satisfaction.

Managing and Measuring Performance

Supply chain operations support service at the counter by physically making the transaction or the experience at the counter possible. Some of the operations include but are not limited to

- information systems platform;
- data management;
- order management;
- distribution;
- inventory management;
- network strategy;
- performance management;
- transportation;
- vendor management.

Many supply chain managers believe that customer satisfaction occurs at the counter. While the experience of the customers with the employees at the "counter" is very important, the whole range of operations behind the counter is important as well. Thus, SCM managers should understand that all the operations that start from raw materials till the product is handed over to the customer, or the service is rendered to the customer, are equally important. Supply chain operations make it possible for customers to have what they want, when they want it, and how they want it.

Pareto Analysis

In addition, SCM techniques can also be applied to service operations. For example, a classic operations management technique used in SCM is the Pareto principle, otherwise known as the 80–20 rule. It applies, in multiple situations, and suggests that 80% of the effects come from 20% of the causes. For example, as a general rule 20% of machine problems will cause 80% of the system errors. Another example in service operations can be seen in that usually 80% of the turnover (i.e., inventory movement) can be ascribed to approximately 20% of the customers, articles, or orders.

Using such a tool a company can

- rank the customers, products, and so on in order of magnitude;
- calculate the percentage that each item contributes to total value;
- derive a cumulative percentage list;
- evaluate the cumulative list and identify appropriate breakpoints (A, B, and C categories).

As an example, take Table 8.1. It helps to identify the customer groups, their primary expectations, and their contribution to total sales.

Note that customer 4 only contributes 6.3% of total sales and their expectations are the most lenient (6 weeks from order to delivery); thus placing them as a category C customer is easily acceptable. While it

Table 8.1. Pareto Customer Analysis

Customer	Sales	% Total Sales	% Cumulative Sales	Products	What the Customer Wants
1	92,000	18.4	18.4	A	3 days ex stock
2	83,500	16.7	35.1	A (75%) B (25%)	2 weeks
3	73,200	14.6	49.7	B	5 days ex stock
4	31,500	6.3	56.0	C	6 weeks order to delivery
Total Sales	500,000				

may seem anathema to rank customers, it is true that not all customers are equal. It may prove both strategically and operationally efficient to choose not to respond to some customer requests. For example, this type of decision would make strategic sense if the volumes of products that are shipped to a particular customer were some of the highest, while the sales value were some of the lowest. Thus, by eliminating this customer, the supply chain has capacity freed up to increase customer service to higher value customers. Of course, it can be argued that the better solution is to develop a supply chain that can supply all customers with high service levels, however, that is not always feasible.

Performance Criteria and Metrics

Other SCM methods can support service operations. Table 8.2 provides several examples of service quality criteria. These are important so that performance metrics can be assessed and monitored so that each dimension of service quality can be aggressively pursued.

Table 8.2. Examples of Service Quality Criteria

Service Quality Dimension	Criteria
Reliability	• Billing accuracy • Order accuracy • On time completion • Promises kept
Responsiveness	• On time appointment • Timely call-back • Timely confirmation of order
Assurance	• Skills of employees • Training provided to employees • Honesty of employees • Reputation of firm
Empathy	• Customized service capabilities • Customer recognition • Degree of server–customer contact • Knowledge of the customer
Tangibles	• Appearance of the employees • Appearance of the facility • Appearance of customers • Equipment and tools used

Once particular criteria have been determined, then specific SCM metrics can be assessed. For example, overall customer service level can be measured as the desired probability versus the actual percentage that product demand can be met from stock. This can be expressed in a number of ways:

- Percentage of orders completely satisfied from stock
- Percentage of units demanded which are met from stock
- Percentage of units demanded which are delivered on time
- Percentage of time there is stock available

Specifically, reliability performance metrics might include percentage of items shipped without errors, percentage of goods delivered on time, and percentage of goods shipped without damage.

Responsiveness might be measured through assessing speed (reduced order-cycle time), flexibility (time required to respond to custom requests), and malfunction recovery (response time to respond to service failures such as the wrong product being shipped).

Balanced Scorecard

One key aspect to remember is that the *entire* supply chain impacts a customer's experience. Thus, it is of even greater importance to view and measure the performance of the supply chain as a whole, rather than just individual components. One way of doing this is through a technique called the balanced scorecard. The balanced *scorecard* is an analytic framework for translating a company's vision and high-level business strategy into specific, quantifiable goals and for monitoring performance against those goals. The methodology breaks high-level strategies into objectives, measurements, targets, and initiatives. It does this by improving an organization's performance in the four general areas of financials, customer perspective, business, and learning processes. This type of analysis is easily tied into SCM. An example can be seen in Figure 8.5.

Robert S. Kaplan and David Norton, who wrote an article about it in 1992 for the *Harvard Business Review*, are usually credited with the idea for the balanced scorecard. Today many companies use one or more

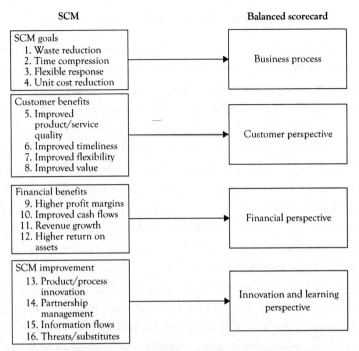

SCM   Balanced scorecard

SCM goals
  1. Waste reduction
  2. Time compression   Business process
  3. Flexible response
  4. Unit cost reduction

Customer benefits
  5. Improved
     product/service
     quality   Customer perspective
  6. Improved timeliness
  7. Improved flexibility
  8. Improved value

Financial benefits
  9. Higher profit margins
  10. Improved cash flows   Financial perspective
  11. Revenue growth
  12. Higher return on
      assets

SCM improvement
  13. Product/process
      innovation   Innovation and learning
  14. Partnership   perspective
      management
  15. Information flows
  16. Threats/substitutes

Figure 8.5. Comparing SCM measures to balanced scorecards.

of its principles without having formally adopted the *balanced scorecard* methodology. As Arthur Schneiderman, an independent business-process management consultant, states, "There are many different *balanced scorecards*, and they serve many different purposes. But most organizations will say its purpose is to link strategy to action."

A key element to a successful service supply chain is tying the customer's perspective to that of the organization; creating and utilizing balanced scorecards can give the organization a tool to do just that. By focusing on the elements discussed in this chapter—focusing on customers, improving personnel, and being culturally sensitive, companies can be ready to confront the cost and performance pressures in the global market that is focusing more and more on service operations as a differentiator. More importantly, they will have the strategic flexibility—the right tools, information, and organizational structure—to help position them for future growth while staying ahead of the pack.

Mini-Case: Southwest Airlines Co.

Southwest Airlines Co. employs a number of balanced *scorecards*, including one which relates ground crew performance to company profitability. Directly relating a financial measure such as "lower costs" with an operations metric like "fast ground turnaround" is a new idea at the Dallas-based airline, says Mike Van de Ven, vice president of financial planning and analysis. "Historically, the budget system was the primary system to monitor costs, and if you were an accountant, you got it," he says. "But if you were an operations person, and you weren't used to cost centers and general ledgers and budget-to-actual variances, it didn't make any sense to you." The operations people had hundreds of metrics dealing with things such as on time performance or baggage delivery, but they weren't linked directly to the financial measures or the budget system, Van de Ven says. "So what we have been doing over the past several years is putting these things together, and that neatly rolls into this *balanced scorecard* concept." Another advantage of this integrated *scorecard* approach is that it retains the hundreds of detailed metrics for front-line supervisors but gives top management a "dashboard" summarizing a few key measures. Van de Ven states, "We are trying to get more focused on key measurements that we want to stay on top of."

Key Take-Aways

- The ultimate goal of any supply chain is to satisfy your customers' needs in a way that is profitable to your company in the long run.
- The "customer experience" is a chain of contacts that the customer undergoes in obtaining a product or service. Managing the customer experience must be done from the customer's perspective throughout the supply chain.
- Service operations in the manufacturing sector are supporting processes such as transport and distribution, administration, maintenance, customer support, and so forth.
- Customer service requires anticipating customer expectations and continually enhancing their experiences.

- Transferring new procedures and concepts to members of another culture are more difficult than may be initially imagined. Also, learning to operate in a new culture involves questioning and articulating previously taken-for-granted beliefs and assumptions.

Reflection Points

1. Does your firm view service operations as a key aspect of SCM or is it viewed as a secondary issue? Do you know if your view of customer service is the same as your managers and employees?

2. One of the key difficulties in service operations can be summed up in this phrase "how do you train people to be nice?" How does your company approach training people to be nice? Do employees have to serve each other well before they can serve the customers well? Do your employees serve each other well?

3. In this chapter it was mentioned that not all customers are equal and that a Pareto analysis can be useful in determining who your most important customers are and which customers might need to be dropped. Do you agree with this viewpoint or do you feel that the customer is always right? Are all customers worthy of keeping as customers? When is the last time you chose to keep an unprofitable customer?

4. What are some of the SCM metrics that your company captures that can be used to support service operations? What metrics in your company can easily be tied to financial results and communicated to employees?

5. What are some opportunities in your organization for balanced scorecards? Have you ever seen the scorecards that your customers keep on you? For example, Wal-Mart scorecards their vendors. If you don't know if your customers keep a scorecard on your performance, ask them. And, if they do, ask if you can learn more about how they are measuring your performance so that you can work together as a team to improve your customer service. If you don't know what your customer wants, it is hard to satisfy them 100% of the time.

Additional Resources

Bolton, R., & Lemon, K. (1999, May). A dynamic model of customers' usage of services: Usage as an antecedent and consequence of satisfaction. *Journal of Marketing Research 36*(2), 171–186.

Carr, A., Muthsamy, S., & Owens, C. (2012). Strategic repositioning of the service supply chain. *Organization Development Journal 30*(1), 63–78.

Frei, F. X. (2006, November). Breaking the trade-off between efficiency and service. *Harvard Business Review 84*(11), 92–101.

Narayanan, V.G., & Raman, A. (2004, November). Aligning incentives in supply chains. *Harvard Business Review 82*(11), 94–102.

CHAPTER 9

Uncertainty

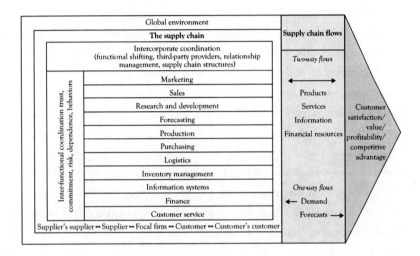

Chapter Objectives

- Expand on the impact of uncertainty in the supply chain as discussed in prior chapters
- Discuss the differences between demand side and supply side uncertainty
- Learn more about the bullwhip effect introduced in Chapter 4 (on forecasting)
- Consider coping strategies for SCM uncertainty
- Review mini-case examples of best practices regarding uncertainty

With today's move toward globalization, firms are managing increasingly complex supply chains of subsidiaries, customers, and suppliers. Information technology (IT) helps manage this complexity either by providing supply chain information, facilitating communication between supply chain partners, or supporting managers' decisions when coordinating these networks. As Kim and Oh[1] put it, "global coordination is one of the most important functions firms have to perform for optimal global operations to achieve operational flexibility."

Alliances all along the supply chain often decide the success or failure of a firm. A basic requirement for a company participating in a supply chain is to open up their own information system for input from upstream and downstream sources. Companies receive information from other members of the chain and disclose their own data to others. Unobstructed information flow, however, with all its positive implications, bears a huge potential of risk. Uncontrollable factors gain importance with the increase of a system's complexity and can occur unexpectedly.

Data received may be misinterpreted and the biased information may be further distributed and amplified throughout the supply chain. As a consequence, long-term planning is extremely difficult and the enlargement of the time horizon increases uncertainty. This chapter will describe certain sources of uncertainty and provide strategies on how to resolve these problems in an attempt to improve the supply chain to the benefit of all participants. The areas of emphasis will be:

- Areas of Uncertainty
- Coping Strategies
- Supplier Relationships
- Seamless Supply Chain
- Best Practices.

Supply Chain Uncertainty

In order to cope with uncertainty within the supply chain a manager must first understand and identify the sources of uncertainty within the various categories and between them. Using the supply-chain operations reference (SCOR) configurational model (see Figure 9.1), we can see that uncertainty and IT issues are not expressly listed.

In general, uncertainty can occur within each of the five categories as part of daily operations. Uncertainty can also exist *between* each of the categories. IT comes into play as a way of coordinating the various categories and reducing the uncertainty. One way of thinking about it is that IT becomes the arrows in the diagram.

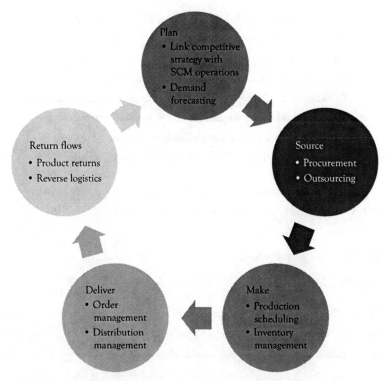

Figure 9.1. Operational categories of supply chain management.
(Adapted from the SCOR Model).

Now, if we wish to categorize the various sources of uncertainty that occur within the supply chain, they can be grouped in the following four areas:

- **Demand side:** This source of uncertainty can be simply explained as the immediate customer. The company responds to the information obtained from the needs of the customers it supplies. As this information flows upstream throughout the various levels of the supply chain the accuracy of the data is distorted and less reliable.
- **Supply side:** Materials, components, and subassemblies supplied by various vendors contribute to this source. Uncertainty stems from the large number of unpredictable possibilities that could disrupt the material flow from suppliers. An example is the 9/11 terrorist attacks on the United States,

which closed the US borders causing JIT deliveries from Canadian and Mexican suppliers to become impossible.

• **Manufacturing process:** This process consists of all of the steps that the company takes to produce the final product. The lack of efficiency in this process can add to uncertainty.

• **Planning and control systems:** These are the systems used to plan and control the supply chain. If these systems are not effectively managed they will also result in increased uncertainty.

Each of these sources of uncertainty leads to various problems in the supply chain. The types of problems are summarized in Table 9.1.

Demand Side Uncertainty

Amplification Effects

One of the main aspects of demand side uncertainty is known as the **Bullwhip effect**, otherwise known as the **amplification effect**, which is simply upstream order magnification.

Table 9.1. Problems with Uncertainty

Uncertainty Source Affected	Cause of Uncertainty: Particular Weaknesses Observed in Real-World Value Stream
Process Side	• No measures of process performance • Reactive rather than proactive maintenance • Random shop floor layout • Interference between value streams
Supply Side	• Short notification of changes to supplier requirement • Excessive supplier delivery lead time • Adversarial supplier relationship • No vendor measures of performances
Demand Side	• No customer stock visibility • Adversarial customer relationship • Large infrequent deliveries to customer • Continuous product modifications causing high levels of obsolescence
Control Side	• Poor stock auditing • No synchronization and poor visibility among adjacent processes • Incorrect supplier lead time in MRP logic • Infrequent MRP runs

Throughout the different levels of the supply chain both information and material flow become distorted. This distortion causes the chain to become more and more inefficient as you progress upstream in the process.

Figure 9.2 illustrates the bullwhip effect and how each level in the supply chain adds a small amount of variance (uncertainty) in how they respond to the initial customer demand. By the time the final orders have reached the production plant, they do not remotely reflect the actual customer demand pattern.

Forrester[2] defined an information-feedback system as one that "exists when the environment leads to a decision that results in action, which affects the environment and thereby influences future decisions." He showed that this feedback mechanism led to an amplification or "bullwhip effect" that is a direct consequence of the dynamics and time-varying behaviors of any industrial organization.

In other words, the very forms and complex information systems structures required to manage a supply chain gives rise to undesirable behaviors.[3] For example, signaling appropriate players of needed changes is difficult because the bullwhip effect creates inaccurate forecast data which is difficult to control.[4] Translating appropriate data into desired forms also produces difficulties because the same basic data can lead to different measurements of the bullwhip effect, depending on the sequence of aggregating these data in the analysis.

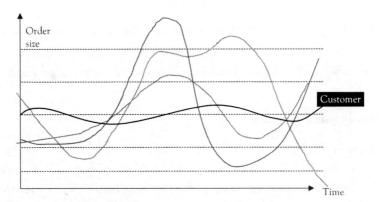

Figure 9.2. Bullwhip effect.[5]

What Are Possible Responses to Amplification Effects?

Information Sharing

One direct response is information sharing among all the members of the supply chain. Lee and Whang found that this information sharing should include sales data, order status (tracking data), sales forecasts, and production/delivery schedules.[6] There is a critical relationship between partial and complete information sharing and inventory system performance.

If your supplier understands why your demand has fluctuated, they don't have to "guess," when they "guess" they insert error into the system. This error escalates as the demand fluctuations flow throughout the supply chain—like ripples on a pond. One small rock can cause many ripples that get bigger the further they move away from the source. This is the essence of the bullwhip effect and demand side uncertainty.

Firms have attempted to integrate these various issues under the rubric of Collaborative Planning, Forecasting, and Replenishment (CPFR), in which all the firms in a supply chain share their inventory and forecasting data. CPFR, however, is a complex system which requires several specific actions at every step; this can be seen in Figure 9.3.

Firms such as Wal-Mart and Dell have used CPFR to great advantage. Currently the Voluntary Inter-industry Commerce Standards (VICS) group provides a website listing best practices for CPFR along with information on implementation strategies.[7]

Utilize New Technology: Such as RFID

If trading partners use RFID it can provide visibility throughout the supply chain. This is another way that information sharing can occur. As we mentioned earlier, the key factor for widespread RFID tag usage is cost.

Supply Side Uncertainty

Demand amplification or bullwhip effects are examples of serial interaction in the supply chain. In other words, a single customer and a single supplier interact between each tier of the supply chain. However, the supplier in each tier also interacts with other channels in the supply chain. These interactions within a single tier are parallel interactions and they

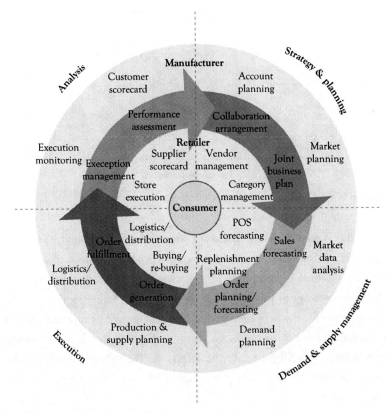

Figure 9.3. CPFR structure.

can directly effect the traditional, serial interactions of a single supply chain.

Parallel Supply Chain Interactions

As an example, Jones found parallel supply chain interactions within an automotive supply chain.[8] Specifically, poor delivery performance and quality from some suppliers directly affected the efficiency of the good JIT suppliers. An example of how this can occur was provided by Wilding and Hill and is shown in Figure 9.4.[9]

Assume a company builds two products, A and B, each requiring the same amount of capacity allocation and being composed of subcomponents W, X, Y, and Z. And assume the demand is 100 units and component part safety stocks are 50 units. As long as JIT deliveries are kept, the entire process remains stable.

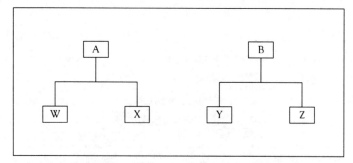

Product structures

Figure 9.4. Product structures.

What if part W is not delivered timely? In all likelihood, the manager will use the safety stock of 50 units to produce 50 units of A. After that, in an effort to keep capacity utilization high, the manager will use the spare capacity to produce 50 extra units of B. Assuming the delayed parts appear for the next time period, the process will be reversed and 50 extra units of A will be produced. Thus at this level, production quickly goes back to equilibrium but the effects on the subsuppliers will take longer to stabilize. The consequences are similar to those of amplification effects and are:

- Suppliers that provide good service and delivery will suffer disruption to their schedules due to suppliers that do not provide their level of service.
- Disruption of planned schedules remote from first tier suppliers can be caused by changes in product mix.
- Customers are frequently unaware of the problems they create for suppliers by small schedule changes.

Concerning parallel uncertainty, Wilding found that suppliers and assemblers could either have their production stopped or their schedule disrupted by parallel interactions up to 18% of the time.[10]

What Are Possible Responses to Parallel Uncertainty Effects?

Intuition would suggest, and research and practice have shown that parallel interactions can be reduced by increasing the amount of inventory in the supply chain. But wait, we don't want more inventory in the system, right? The goal of SCM is to minimize the inventory within the pipeline. Additionally, increasing inventories increases the amount of amplification uncertainty in the supply chain.

Here again we see that the role of SCM is complex, yet critical to the organization. Trade-offs must be analyzed and considered in light of your business goals, strategy, processes, suppliers, and customers.

Manufacturing Process Uncertainty

Within the manufacturing system, there are numerous areas of uncertainty associated with the various manufacturing processes. One example is the use of MRP systems and the problem of limited planning horizons (which is why MRP systems are frozen after certain time periods).

Four distinct areas have been identified where manufacturing issues can cause uncertainty and actually exasperate the amplification or bullwhip effect:[11]

- **Demand forecast updating**—where increasing safety stock in the pipeline causes erroneous amplification of demand in the supply chain.
- **Order batching**—where customers tend to order goods during particular times. For example, the manufacturer may get large bulk orders followed by long periods of low demand based on changing order patterns from its customers. Communication is key to understanding the changes.
- **Price fluctuations**—where promotions and "loss leaders" cause surges in demand. This is caused by customer buying more products sooner than they usually would (this is referred to as forward buying).
- **Rationing and shortage gaming**—where retailers submit multiple orders when supply is scarce. The idea is that by submitting multiple orders above their actual requirements, that they will receive what they actually need. If the manufacturer doesn't know what is happening, this seeming increase to demand will affect its future forecasts and potentially cause overstocking.

What Are Possible Responses to Manufacturing Process Uncertainty Effects?

Each of these effects can be resolved through communication. First, the anomaly in ordering patterns, consumption, and so on must be identified. Once the change is identified the responsible manager can investigate and inquire as to the causes. The primary goal for the manager is first to implement internal control mechanisms to identify changes, such as some sort of statistical process control as is used in quality management. If the issue is not identified it cannot be isolated and investigated. The change should not be assumed, normal course of business, without first insuring that is truly the case.

It is a common occurrence, in our experience, that fluctuations in demand due to promotions are not systematically tracked. This causes future forecasts to be erroneous. For example, let's consider a consumer products manufacturer that agrees to run a promotion in conjunction with a customer in the spring of 2013. This promotion causes demand for the promotional product to be increased above normal demand. If this promotional activity is not captured systematically, it will erroneously increase the forecast for that item in the next period, or even as far out as the spring of 2014.

Planning and Control Systems

Although huge amounts of money have been spent on IT to coordinate the various members of supply chains, the technology has its limitations. One of the fallacies of traditional long-term planning and forecasting and its traditional modeling tools is that they are incapable of predicting discontinuities (i.e., major nonlinearities, an extreme example being the 9/11 attacks).[12] While certain repetitive or seasonal patterns may be easily predictable, other issues such as technological innovations or price increases are not.

Recent work has differentiated the uncertainty into four levels:[13]

- A clear-enough future
- Alternative future

- A range of futures
- True ambiguity

Various types of uncertainties impact the planning forecast at each of these four uncertainty levels. For example, if incorrect data is being represented, then this impacts the robustness of any of the tool sets being used to solve a problem. Overall, these uncertainties interact to such a point that a long range forecast/model in the "range of futures" or "total ambiguity" stage can become nothing more than a "gut instinct" call on the part of the decision maker. This is not to say that this type of forecasting is unforgiveable, it is simply a reality and falls under the category of qualitative forecasting that we mentioned earlier.

Coping Strategies for Supply Chain Uncertainty

In the previous sections, we provided some basic strategies for responding to specific types of uncertainty. In this section we delve deeper into methods of responding to uncertainty. Specifically, we focus on those strategies and methods that respond to uncertainty while focusing on the supply chain as a whole. This framework can be seen in Figures 9.5 and 9.6.

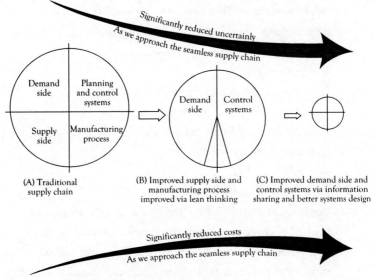

Figure 9.5. Uncertainty coping strategies.[14]

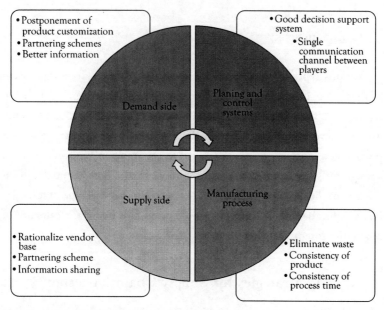

Figure 9.6. Final issues in coping with uncertainty.

The general mode of attack is to address these issues in this order:

1. **Manufacturing process and supply side**
   - Implement "Lean Thinking" into the manufacturing process: Lean Thinking is a concept that deals with eliminating all the waste and inefficiency within a process.
   - Continuously improve relationships with suppliers: The goal is to integrate them into the supply chain so that they know exactly what you need from them to be successful together.

2. **Demand side and control systems**
   - Information sharing is key: The best strategy is to use one method of communication with suppliers and allow them direct access to consumer information. This will enable them to be proactive rather than reactive. This will also add value to the overall supply chain and reduce the magnitude

of the bullwhip effect. There must be a system in place with timely accurate information available for planning and decision making.

- ○ Address interdepartmental coordination: Ensure that internal information flows are planned, expected, and working properly. Do not make the mistake of assuming that the "left hand knows what the right hand is doing." Get out of your office and see for yourself that everyone is working from the same game plan.

Supply Chain Partnerships

Uncertainty in the supply chain impacts the performance of all the trading partners up and down the chain. To cope with such uncertainties in the supply chain, firms can create an alliance with its suppliers. As discussed in earlier, firms can attain their competitive advantage by working closely with their suppliers.

Traditionally, American and European firms have been using a large pool of suppliers to increase their bargaining power in terms of lower costs, higher quality, and faster delivery times. In recent times, firms have focused on reducing the supplier base since the close association with specific suppliers can lead to relationship-based discounts. Most of these trends toward a smaller supplier base have been fueled by the success of Japanese firms, which recognize the strategic buyer–supplier partnerships as a critical factor for success.

The benefits of partnerships to buyer firms in the form of lower cost and higher quality have been widely cited in the literature. Generally, there is a notion that suppliers lose out in partnerships with buyers. Suppliers, however, also benefit from adopting the strategy of maintaining partnerships with the buyer firms as compared to using a transactional approach to servicing customers. A list of the benefits of supplier relationships is summarized in Table 9.2.

As we have discussed previously, forming a partnership is not an easy task since it requires a significant attitudinal, as well as, structural change on the part of both partners. Selecting the right partner from a pool of alternatives is a challenging task, which requires considering the issues

Table 9.2. Benefits of Supplier Partnerships[15]

Benefits for Buyers	Cost Savings
Cost	Economies of scale
Quantity discounts	Ordering
High quality	Production
Improved timing	Transportation
Benefits for Suppliers	
Market	Administrative
Understanding of customer needs	Switching
	Process integration
Benefits for Both	
Convergent expectation and goals	Joint products and process development
Reduced effects from externalities	Improved communication
Reduced opportunism	Shared risk and rewards

of compatibility in terms of culture and management styles. Sustaining a supply chain partnership requires a fair amount of cooperation, trust, and goodwill between the partners. When cooperation, trust, and goodwill are there, however, you can work together to form a seamless supply chain.

The Seamless Supply Chain

Achieving world-class delivery precision is one of the most demanding and challenging goals of customer-oriented end producers and their suppliers. Designing and operating efficient supply chains are major requirements for delivery precision. Common wisdom holds that the markets will force companies to build and operate highly efficient supply chains, but the entire supply chain is important—not just an individual company. The seamless supply chain is a perfect flow of information and materials facilitated by all supply chain partners. This supply chain can only be reached by reducing sources of uncertainty throughout the extended supply chain. Today, people expend significant effort to expedite orders, check order status frequently, deploy inventory, "just in case" pad lead times, or find other creative ways to buffer themselves against disruptive events. A recent survey on supply chain management issues showed that nearly 40% of the surveyed companies are currently preparing to implement various supply chain management tools, technology, or both. But fewer than 10% of them have actually implemented smooth material flow principles that will support successful supply chain management.

There is a strong relationship between the best-in-class supply chain practices and levels of supply chain uncertainty. The following is the summary of closely related best practices:

- **Simplicity:** This involves the adoption of the already proven solutions such as inventory reduction, simplified products and processes, flexibility, and commitment to continuous and incremental improvement.
- **Smooth material flow:** To establish a smooth material flow along the value stream so that a product proceeds from design to launch, from order to delivery, and from raw materials to a finished product in the hands of the customer with no stoppages, scrap, or backflows.
- **Value stream management:** This makes sure that products move in a more effective fashion, from concept to launch, from order to delivery, and from sourcing of raw materials to delivery to the customer.
- **Lean thinking:** As discussed, this is a philosophy that seeks to shorten the time between customer order and product delivery by eliminating sources of waste and delay.

Of course, by virtue of the fact that these are best practices, most firms are not performing at this level. So how does a supply chain manager assess how close they are to these best practices and whether they are making progress? One way is to determine what stage of supply chain maturity they are at and with it, how well they can manage uncertainty.

Stages of Supply Chain Maturity and Uncertainty

The Stevens Reference Framework divides supply chain evolution into four levels:

- **Level one (Baseline):** Companies engage in reactive short-term planning and "firefighting." They have large pools of inventory and are vulnerable to market changes.

- **Level two (Functional integration):** Companies focus inward on goods and are reactive toward their customers.
- **Level three (Internal integration):** All work processes are integrated and the planning process reaches from the customers back to the supplier.
- **Level four (External integration):** The organization achieves integration with all suppliers and synchronizes material flows to form an extended enterprise.

Once a company has determined its stage of supply chain integration and the type of uncertainty to be reduced, it should look for the causes of uncertainty. The process of supply chain reengineering continues until external integration and best-in-class status is reached. The result is a plan taken by the best firms. The plan lays out the steps that a typical company would take in improving its supply chain operations.

Benefits of Reducing Uncertainty

- Increased visibility
- Remove operational drag
- Improve performance of an organization
- Decrease cost
- Increase market share and profitability
- Reduce inventory

Mini-Case: Best Practices

Digital Equipment

To squash competition from direct vendors and expand a seamless supply chain, Digital used a final assembly model to lower the total supply-chain cost and improve product delivery time with flexibility in obtaining customized PCs.

Although the base systems and core components owned by Digital will sit in Hall-Mark's warehouse until an order is received, the units will be "kitted" to sport the exact hardware options sought by a reseller. Once assembled, the PCs will be tested and loaded with the factory-installed software. This is an instance of process uncertainty fix with value-added warehouses. A Digital-employed asset manager will ensure that each system is suitable for sale. In exchange for this work, Digital will pay Hall-Mark an undisclosed assembly fee. Hall-Mark officials say this program will better position its resellers to meet customer needs such as building to users' specifications and turning around an order within a day's time.

Cisco

Cisco's model of building a seamless supply chain is one that many companies can follow. It proves that you do not have to own or control most of the elements in your supply chain, yet have complete visibility of the chain. The Internet allows companies to coordinate more closely with their suppliers and also enables just-in-time delivery that lets businesses greatly reduce inventories. Cisco's suppliers build and ship while Cisco handles all of financial transactions. This is an excellent instance of control/demand uncertainty fix.

Ford

Ford and its suppliers are following Cisco's lead for reduced inventories and inefficiencies, faster transactions, and shorter order to payment cycles. Ford is giving its suppliers greater responsibility for building whole modules to be assembled in finished cars. Ford's push to E-business is to trigger mass customization where a customer configures his car through the company's website with greater brand choices. Also, supply chains are being built within the supply chain where suppliers and customers are reaping benefits alike. This is an instance of demand/supply uncertainty fix.

Dell

Dell is another instance where all the hardware/software can be configured online. Vendors manage the inventories while Dell only builds the final assembly and has strategically placed its suppliers close to its geographical proximity to avoid delays.

Benetton

Italian clothes manufacturer, Benetton, used postponement as its strategy to buffer for color demand uncertainty. With an IT-integrated supply chain, capturing point of sale data, the mainframe in Italy knew instantly what the demand at any time was. It had its yarn knitted into sweaters and postponed the process of dyeing until it received the order. Thus, it could ship the orders to customers within 3 weeks.

Key Take-Aways

- Supply chain uncertainty can be broken into four categories: demand side, supply side, manufacturing processes, and planning and control systems. Breaking down uncertainty into categories allows you to understand the sources generating the uncertainty and allow you to address it systematically and proactively.
- The Bullwhip Effect is a significant contributor to supply chain uncertainty. Strategic information sharing with suppliers and customers can allow the firm to control the variability associated with this amplification of errors effect within the supply chain.
- There are coping strategies that allow companies to address uncertainty and its effects. These include, but are not limited to, lean thinking, building relationships with suppliers, information sharing throughout the value chain, and improving interdepartmental coordination.
- Best practices to address supply chain uncertainty include simplicity, smooth material flow, value stream management, and lean thinking.

Reflection Points

1. What other benefits, besides those mentioned in this chapter, would your company get if uncertainty is reduced within your supply chain? Any uncertainty within your supply chain affects many other aspects of your company's health and vitality—what health benefits do you foresee for support functions within your organization if uncertainty

is reduced in the supply chain? These types of benefits, those that affect the support systems within organizations are often forgotten. Be sure to consider them when weighing options.

2. When you think about the uncertainty experienced by your company—is it primarily externally or internally generated? Do you have processes in place to differentiate between the two?

3. What can you, your team, or both, do to address each of the best practices mentioned? Which of these four do you believe is the most important to reducing uncertainty within your supply chain? Why? Can you think of any "low hanging fruit" that you could address and get a quick win in this arena?

Additional Resources

Christopher, M. (2000). *Managing the global supply chain in an uncertain world.* London, UK: Probity Research.

De Meyer, A., Loch, C. H., & Pich, M. T. (2002, Winter). Managing project uncertainty: From variation to chaos. *MIT Sloan Management Review* 60–67.

Dhillon, G., & Ward, J. (2002). Chaos theory as a framework for studying information systems. *Information Resources Management Journal 15*(2), 5–13.

Egelhoff, W. G. (1991). Information-processing theory and the multinational enterprise. *Journal of International Business Studies 22*(3), 341–369.

Geary, S., Childerhouse, P., & Towill, D. R. (2002, July/August). Uncertainty and the seamless supply chain. *Supply Chain Management Review 6*(4), 52–59.

Lee, H. L. (2002). Aligning supply chain strategies with product uncertainties. *California Management Review 44*(3), 105–119.

Lee, H. L., Padmanabhan, V., & Whang, S. (1997). The bullwhip effect in supply chains. *Sloan Management Review 38*(3), 93-102.

Levy, D. (1994, Summer). Chaos theory and strategy: Theory, application and managerial implications. *Strategic Management Journal 15*, 167–178.

Omar, A., Davis-Sramek, B., Myers, M., & Mentzer, J. (2012). A global analysis of orientation, coordination and flexibility in supply chains. *Journal of Business Logistics 33*(2), 128–144.

Shore, B. (2001). Information sharing in global supply chain systems. *Journal of Global Information Technology Management 4*(3), 27–50.

Sterman, J. D. (1989). Modeling managerial behavior: Misperceptions of feedback in a dynamic decisions making experiment. *Management Science 35*(3), 321–339.

Sterman, J. D. (2001). System dynamics modeling: Tools for learning in a complex world. *California Management Review 43*(4), 8–25.

van der Horst, J. G. A. J., & Beulens, A. J. M. (2002). Identifying sources of uncertainty to generate supply chain redesign strategies. *International Journal of Physical Distribution & Logistics Management 32*(6), 409–430.

Wilding, R. D. (1998). The supply chain complexity triangle: Uncertainty generation in the supply chain. *International Journal of Physical Distribution & Logistics Management 28*(8), 599–616.

Wilding, R. D. (1998). Chaos theory: Implications for supply chain management. *The International Journal of Logistics Management 9*(1), 43–56.

SECTION 3

The Future

CHAPTER 10

Future SCM Trends

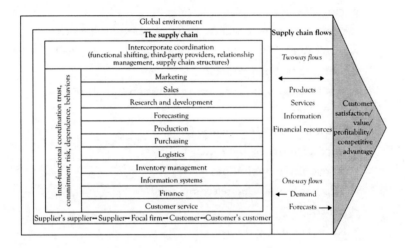

Chapter Objectives

- Assess the continued use of information sharing
- Review the trend from vertical to virtual integration
- Examine the continued growth of reverse logistics

Current SCM Trends

It is important to realize that the current drivers of change in the supply chain will continue to impact organizations at all levels of the supply chain in the foreseeable future. Just as important is to acknowledge that these processes are simply a part of an everchanging system. It is not good enough to understand today's issues without addressing the future impacts of these changes, such as evolving technology, economic issues, and so forth. We have addressed earlier some of what we call today's trends. They include:

- actual customer demand: speed, flexibility, and competitive pricing;
- the outsourcing trend will continue to increase and evolve;
- new software: ERP, sophisticated application software will continue to be implemented;
- new technologies will continue to be used to supply product information:
  - Electronic Data Interchange (EDI)
  - Internet, intranet, and extranet
  - Wireless communications
  - Teleconferencing and telecommuting
  - Bar coding
  - Radio Frequency ID (RFID).

These issues are just a continuation of topics that firms are currently addressing. There are other trends, however, that are just beginning to be seen now which will increase in the near future. Thus, there is always a need to assess new future trends.

One set of trends arises from the logical implications of the four global forces.

- Integration of extended international activities into a coordinated global system.
- Restructuring the global supply chain network to avoid duplicated processes.
- Global expansion of small and medium sized firms.

Another set of trends comes directly from this increase in global competition. Specifically, there will continue to be an intensification of traffic in global logistics channels. The implications are:

- Straining infrastructure capacity in many areas

- Every mode of transportation will be affected
- Effects: congestion, bottlenecks, longer delivery times, reduced transport reliability
- Results: higher costs, diminished effectiveness

There is an additional European trend and that will eventually affect US firms as well, the rapid growth of return flows. This is caused by several reasons including, but not limited to, environmental awareness (greening of the supply chain), more aggressive sales techniques, and an imbalance between flows at an international level.

Shift from Vertical to Virtual Integration

Henry Ford pushed for vertical integration. In other words, he wished to own the entire value chain required to build a car. His thinking was that by doing this, he could reduce waste and increase efficiencies. At its peak, Ford's rubber plantations, steel mills, ships, railroads, and manufacturing facilities could convert raw materials to a car in seven days; however, this required huge amounts of capital and a complex administration. Companies cannot have core competencies that include every aspect of their supply chain. Any process or function of an organization that is not a core competency is one that can cause inefficiency. Additionally, those areas that are not core competencies can be strategically outsourced. Some firms have taken this trend to an extreme where most functions are outsourced.

Outsourcing processes or functions that are not core competencies can relieve the capital requirements of vertical integration while still keeping many of the benefits. Firms that adopt this type of strategy are called virtual companies. Nike is an example of a virtual firm. It consists only of two main sectors: marketing and R&D. Everything else, including logistics, warehousing, manufacturing, and so forth are outsourced. Other firms are following the example of Nike and outsourcing other aspects of their business. In addition to traditionally outsourced functions such as logistics and manufacturing, virtual firms are outsourcing knowledge processes as well. These include functions such as process design and information technology. As firms move to virtual integration, management must realize three important aspects of making the transition:

- First, managers must get used to managing assets, activities, and people they do not control. In many cases in the global environment, managers will never meet the people who performance they must monitor.
- Second, moving to a virtual organization takes time as partner firms in the supply chain must work to reduce duplication and redundancy.
- Third, management must move beyond interacting with suppliers to working with suppliers' suppliers. These parallel supply chain issues must be addressed when managing the overall organization.

Continued Emphasis on Information Sharing

As more information system technologies are implemented there will continue to be a greater emphasis on sharing information within members of the supply chain. Increased information sharing allows firms to reduce chaos and uncertainty effects, forecast more accurately, and respond quickly to system changes. The potential cost savings and enhanced services are significant. There are several key issues and trends that impact this implementation goal.

1. Sharing information openly requires a high degree of trust between the firms. This is sometimes limited when in the case of a large firm that requires smaller suppliers to implement technologies for information sharing which provides the greatest benefits for the larger firm. An example is Wal-Mart requiring all its suppliers to implement EDI in the 1980s.
2. Some firms will not share forecast or planning data under any circumstances. This limits the type of integration a virtual company might wish for.
3. Desire for shared information is beginning to take novel forms, such as the sharing of employees and cross-functional teams.

4. In some cases, the sharing of information may actually be legally limited. For example, in the Federal Government's view, there is a fine line between sharing information to improve forecasts and fixing prices. Thus, changes in political administrations can have immediate impacts on this trend.

Move from Managerial Accounting to Value-Based Accounting

In the wake of the Enron scandal, firms have become aware of the limitations of Generally Accepted Accounting Procedures (GAAP). During the past decade, many firms have moved to managerial accounting practices such as activity-based costing. The benefits of these changes have encouraged firms to look at ways to assess how their work impacts shareholder value. This has led to the adoption of Economic Value Added (EVA) and Market Value Added (MVA) tools. These types of tools lend themselves to being used with the information readily available from ERP systems. This is being driven by the fact that managers are being forced to show how supply chain changes affect the overall health of the firm.

Focus on Security

In the wake of 9/11, security has become a major SCM issue. Railroads, ocean shippers, and trucking companies have had to spend large amounts of time and money in efforts to increase the security of cargo and to make sure that cargo is not used for terrorism. The driver for these activities is both ethical and for legal protection. The official requirements for individual supply chain companies remains in flux as federal legal requirements are continually changing and as new security technologies are being developed. Sadly however, the impact of this particular trend will continue to grow, as the world becomes an increasingly dangerous place to conduct business.

Reverse Logistics

Reverse Logistics (RL) is a process in which a manufacturer systematically accepts previously shipped products or parts from the point for consumption for possible recycling, remanufacturing, resale, or disposal. Thus, a RL system incorporates a supply chain that has been redesigned to manage the backward flow of products or parts destined for remanufacturing, recycling, resale, or disposal.

The management of RL processes breaks down into two general areas: product returns and product packaging. Product returns are heavily driven by customer returns and vary in volume by industry. Product packaging involves recycling of cardboard, plastic, and other packaging material to reduce disposal costs. Processes involved in RL include collection of used, damaged, unwanted, or outdated products as well as packaging and shipping materials.

RL isn't a new concept, but it is an increasingly important one. "Returns have existed from the first time anyone manufactured product or opened a store," says Buzzy Wyland, president of manufacturing services with third party logistics provider (3PL) Genco Distribution. "What's changed—and, it was about ten years ago—is that people started to focus on the real costs involved in returns, which evolved into reverse logistics." Those costs become an issue when returns become a problem. "Most companies have never given reverse logistics much focus," says John McVicker, Genco's VP-customer start-ups. "Some may be aware

Industry	Return Percentage
Magazine publishing	50
Book publishers	20–30
Book distributors	10–20
Greeting cards	20–30
Catalog retailers	18–35
Electronic distributors	10–12
Computer manufacturers	10–20
CD-ROMS	18–25
Printers	4–8
Mail order computer manufacturers	2–5
Mass merchandiser	4–15
Consumer electronics	4–5
Household chemicals	2–3
Auto industry (Parts)	4–6

that reverse logistics was a problem, but most are focused on the sales end of their business and disregard the returns piece." In order to compare the return demands of various industries, refer to the following table.

To better conceptualize the business dimension here, consider the auto industry (parts segment) listed last in the table. While that 4–6% rate of returns may seem low, 90–95% of all automobile starters and alternators sold for replacement in the United States are remanufactured. The Auto Parts Remanufactures Association estimates the market for remanufactured parts to be $36 billion.

So should you be concerned with RL? On one hand, there are no legal requirements for it in the United States, although there is in Europe. While there are no legal requirements to induce US companies to adopt RL systems, there may be operational reasons. Specifically, there are symptoms in operations that returns have become a problem. According to Dr. Richard Dawe with the Fritz Institute of International Logistics those are:

- Returns arriving faster than processing or disposal
- Large amount of returns inventory held in the warehouse
- Unidentified or unauthorized returns
- Lengthy cycle processing times
- Unknown total cost of the returns process
- Customers have lost confidence in the repair activity.

While the symptoms of problem returns can be applied across products and industries, solutions to managing RL are not as general. Unique product dispositions will require different companies to use different reverse logistics techniques. However, the goal for everyone is the same: get the highest value possible from returned items.

Types of Reverse Logistics Systems

Designing and developing a RL supply chain is different from forward logistics in several ways. Differences include the supply chain composition and structure (new parties may be involved and new roles assumed by existing parties, and the forward network may be different from the

RL network); additional government constraints; rapid timing and uncertainty in the environment.

To date, a great deal of RL network research has been done, mostly in Europe. This research has addressed topics as varied as

- recycling steel byproducts;
- sand recycling;
- electronic equipment collection and remanufacturing;
- carpet recycling; and
- a general model investigating the various effects of environmental variables on return flows.

One of the more prolific researchers in RL is M. Fleischmann. He has proposed a generic RL network model based on a mixed integer linear program and presented a continuous optimization model for RL network design. Most important for our discussion here is that he has devised a framework of three typical RL network structures: RL networks for bulk recycling, remanufacturing, and reuse. This provides a useful way of viewing RL networks and allows us an overview of the various requirements of different types of systems.

As an example of how to apply this we will look at carpet recycling. Carpet recycling clearly falls into the bulk-recycling category, which is characterized by substantial initial RL investment costs relative to the product value (low value density), as well as, a high vulnerability with respect to uncertainty in the supply volume. The network structure is

Overview of RL Network Types (based on Fleischman)

	Bulk Recycling	Remanufacturing	Reuse
Structure	• Centralized • Flat • Open loop • Branch-wide cooperation	• Decentralized • Multilevel • Closed loop • No branch cooperation	• Decentralized • Flat • Closed loop • No branch cooperation
Generation	New reverse networks	Extension of forward networks	Extension of forward networks
Ownership	Third parties, material suppliers, OEMs	Mostly OEMs	OEMs, third parties

often flat and centralized at the recycling stage due to the expensive recycling equipment. The system is open loop, meaning that the recycling activities do not interfere with new product sales. Cooperation within the industry often takes place, probably to ensure input volumes. It is easy to see that carpet recycling closely matches this category, making the volume and variability of recyclable carpet a problem of prime importance. In addition to affecting economics, the uncertainty in the quantity and timing or product returns often leads to increased difficulties in planning for RL as compared to forward logistics.

Global Comparison of Reverse Logistics

As mentioned earlier Europe has laws requiring RL systems for manufacturing. This is due to the fact that in Europe there is a great deal of environmental awareness of the depletion of natural resources. This leads to an awareness of customers for green branding and new markets for returned goods. Another reason is cost minimization. Companies that use RL, coupled with recycling or remanufacturing, have been estimated to save 40–60% of the cost of manufacturing a completely new product. Finally, European firms are becoming aware that using RL may cut down delivery lead times, for example, if service parts or, more generally, complex components are remanufactured rather than manufactured from scratch. All of this has led to more research and applications in this area. The laws that have been implemented requiring the recycling of many types of goods effectively increase and stabilize return flows of products.

In the United States, the main environmental driver for some industries is the need to reduce the amount of material going into landfills. An example of this is the carpet industry. Increasingly, local governments are looking to reduce landfill use and putting pressure on manufacturers to take steps toward source reduction. In 2000, 5.1 billion pounds of waste carpet were landfilled in the United States, costing over $90 million just in dumping fees. Moreover, federal, state/provincial, and municipal governments in North America have started implementing energy management programs, as part of which they promote the purchase of carpet with at least 25% recycled content. As a result, US carpet manufacturers signed a memorandum of agreement in 2002, making it a target to divert 40% of carpet waste flow from landfills by 2012. Between 20 and 25% of all used carpet will be recycled. This requires the setup of a RL system to handle the collection of used carpet, the separation of carpet components, and the redistribution of recyclable materials to carpet manufacturers. First attempts at this have been made in the sector of commercial carpets, and the willingness exists to sell recycled carpets in the consumer market.

Unlike forward logistics, however, RL operations are complex and prone to a high degree of uncertainty, affecting collection rates, recycling lead times, and capacities in the reverse channel. Part of this uncertainty lies in the fact that the physical distances that RL networks in the United States must cover are much larger than in Europe with its higher population densities. Thus, US carpet manufacturers and other players in the RL chain are interested in knowing how to best structure their reverse logistics systems and what operational difficulties they will have to face.

Focus on Application

Reverse logistics is practiced in many industries, including those producing steel, commercial aircraft, computers, automobiles, chemicals, appliances, and medical items. Companies that have practiced reverse logistics include BMW, Delphi, DuPont, General Motors, Hewlett-Packard, Storage Tek, and TRW. Reverse logistics is also widely used in the automobile industry. It provides automobile firms with far-reaching cost and strategic advantages in a highly competitive industry. BMW's strategic goal is to design a "totally reclaimable" automobile in the first half of the 21st century. Its objective is to recover, recondition, and then reuse all parts. The effective use of reverse logistics can help a firm to compete in its industry, especially when confronting intense competition and low profit margins.

Key Take-Aways

- Trends reflect continued increases in information sharing supporting virtual integration and demanding increased support from IT foundations.

- Security is increasing in importance not only for international, but also domestic supply chain activities.
- Reverse logistics continues to increase in importance. Companies that do not address this area will weaken their competitive position in the marketplace as others strengthen in themselves in the reverse supply chain.

Reflection Points

1. How can you help steer your company toward the future? What type of future trend analysis do you have in place in your firm? How far into the future do you plan and look for trends: 5 years, 10 years, or 20 years?
2. In your particular industry, what are the drivers that have limited or supported RL development?
3. Does your organization proactively manage its reverse supply chain? If not, why not? Could optimizing your reverse supply chain give you a strategic advantage over your competition?

Additional Resources

Donovan, J. (2003). RF identification tags: Show me the money. *Electronic Engineering Times* 41.

Elllis, S., & Lambright, S. (2002). Real time tech—Unilever sees intelligent product tags as the brains behind real-time supply chains. *Optimize* 44.

Gilliland, M., & Prince, D. (2001). New approaches to "unforecastable" demand. *Journal of Business Forecasting Methods & Systems 20*(2), 9–13.

Karkkainen, M., & Holmstrom, J. (2002). Wireless product identification: Enabler for handling efficiency, customisation and information sharing. *Supply Chain Management: An International Journal 7*(4), 242–252.

Lee, H. L. (2010, October). Don't tweak your supply chain—rethink it end to end. *Harvard Business Review 88*(10), 62–69.

Murray, C. J. (2003). Emerging markets—"smart" data sets. *Electronic Engineering Times* 38.

O'Connell, A. (2007, November). Improve your returns on returns. *Harvard Business Review 85*(11), 30–34.

Prokesch, S. (2010). The sustainable supply chain. *Harvard Business Review 88*(10), 70–72.

Reader's Notes

As you may have noticed while reading the book, many of the readings listed at the end of the chapter were not from the latest journal articles. This was a deliberate choice. This book is intended for mid to upper level executives who are NOT supply chain management professionals but need to have a better understanding of key components of SCM so that they can support their company's competitive issues. As such, it is expected that you will be interacting with the supply chain directors within your company. Most, if not all of these individuals will have come through the ranks over the course of years. Thus, the authors chose to include articles that have been used by professionals throughout the past several years. The goal is to help you understand how the profession has adapted over time. However, for those of you wish to look at current issues, now and in the future, we suggest the following:

Organizations

CSCMP: Council of Supply Chain Management Professionals. (http://cscmp .org/) Formerly the Council of Logistics Management (CLM), they refer to themselves as the world's leading source for the supply chain management profession. They provide excellent conferences and published materials on various SCM topics.

ISM: Institute for Supply Management (http://www.ism.ws/). This is another key SCM group that also focuses on purchasing. Many non-SCM executives are familiar with ISM due to their Manufacturing reports which are used as economic indicators.

Researchers

Dr. Martin Christopher, SCM Researcher, Cranfield University. Dr. Christopher has published books and article on logistics, SCM and relationship marketing. Of potential use to many executives is the fact that they have been translated into most of the major languages worldwide.

Dr. Hau Lee, SCM Researcher, Stanford University. While some of his articles are primarily for researchers any of his Harvard Business Reviews articles provide keen insights in SCM issues.

Dr. John T. (Tom) Mentzer, University of Tennessee. Although recently deceased, Dr. Mentzer wrote over 8 books and 190 articles during his career. He was the most prolific author in the Journal of Business Logistics, which provide articles that executives will find readable and informative.

Dr. David Simchi-Levi, SCM Researcher, MIT. While many of his articles are heavily mathematical, they provide useful insights into designing SCM networks. His supply chain textbook is used throughout the country.

Notes

Chapter 1

1. Mark Twain, Letter to George Bainton, 10/15/1888.
2. Mentzer (2001).
3. Porter (1980).
4. Superquinn's CEO, Feargal Quinn: LaBarre, P. (2001, November). Leader— Feargal Quinn. *Fast Company* 52, 88.

Chapter 3

1. The description of the term or behavior "to cherish" is adapted from the definition and synonyms provided at dictionary.com on May 25, 2012.

Chapter 4

1. Chopra and Meindl.

Chapter 5

1. http://www.bearingpoint.com

Chapter 9

1. Kim and Oh (2000).
2. Forrester (1961).
3. Lee, Padmanabhan, and Whang (1997).
4. Taylor (2000).
5. Source: McGruffy (1998).
6. Lee and Whang (1998).
7. Information is available at http://www.vics.org/committees/cpfr/
8. Jones (1990).
9. Wilding and Hill (1999).
10. Wilding (1998).
11. Lee (1997).
12. Mintzberg (1994).

13. Courtney et al. (1997).
14. From Mason-Jones and Towill (2000).
15. Adapted from Maloni and Benton (1997).

References

Chopra, S., & Meindl, P. (2004). *Supply chain management: Strategy, planning and operation* (2nd ed.). Upper Saddle River, NJ: Pearson.

Courtney, H., Kirkland, J., & Viguerie, P. (1997). Strategy under uncertainty. *Harvard Business Review 75*(6), 67–82.

Chopra, S., & Meindl, P. (2001). *Supply chain management: Strategy, planning and operations.* Prentice-Hall, Upper Saddle River, NJ.

Forrester, J. W. (1961). *Industrial dynamics,* MIT Press, Cambridge, Mass.

Jones, M. P. (1990). An investigation into the logistical performance of a partially just-in-time supply chain by the application of discrete event simulation. Thesis, University of Warwick.

Kim, B., & Oh, H. (2000). An exploratory inquiry into the perceived effectiveness of a global information system. *Information Management & Computer Security 8*(3).

Kim, B., & Oh, H. (2005). The impact of decision making sharing between supplier and manufacturer on their collaboration performance, *Supply Chain Management: An International Journal 11*(3–4), 223–236.

Lee, H. L., & Whang, S. (1998). *Information sharing in a supply chain.* Stanford, CA: Graduate School of Business, Stanford University.

Lee, H. L. (2002). Aligning supply chain strategies with product uncertainties. *California Management Review 44*(3), 105–119.

Lee, H. L., Padmanabhan, V., & Whang, S. (1997). Information distortion in a supply chain: The bullwhip effect. *Management Science 43*(4), 546–558.

Maloni, M. J., & Benton, W. C. (1997). Supply chain partnerships: Opportunities for operations research. *European Journal of Operations Research 101*(3), 419–429.

Mason-Jones, R., & Towill, D. R. (2000). Coping with uncertainty: Reducing "bullwhip" behavior in global supply chains. *Supply Chain Forum 1*, 40–45.

McGruffy, T. (1998). Electronic Commerce and Value Chain Management.

Mentzer, J. T. (2001). *Supply chain management.* Thousands Oak, California: Sage.

Mentzer, J. T. (2004). *Fundamentals of supply chain management: Twelve drivers of competitive advantage.* Sage Publications, Th ousand Oaks. Ca.

Mintzberg, H. (1994). Rethinking strategic planning part I: Pitfalls and fallacies. *Long Range Planning 27*(3), 12–21.

Mintzberg, H. (1994, January–February). The rise and fall of strategic planning. *Harvard Business Review.*

Porter, M. (1980). *Competitive Advantage.* New York, NY: Free Press.

Taylor, D. H. (2000). Demand amplification: Has it got us beat? *International Journal of Physical Distribution & Logistics Management 30*(6), 515–533.

Wilding, R. D., & Hill, J. F. (1999). *Parallel Interactions in Supply Chains*. 2nd International Symposium on Advanced Manufacturing Processes, Systems and Technologies, AMPST 99.

Wilding, R. D. (1998). The supply chain complexity triangle: Uncertainty generation in the supply chain. *International Journal of Physical Distribution & Logistics Management 28*(8), 599–616.

Index

Announcing the Business Expert Press Digital Library

Concise E-books Business Students Need for Classroom and Research

This book can also be purchased in an e-book collection by your library as

- a one-time purchase,
- that is owned forever,
- allows for simultaneous readers,
- has no restrictions on printing, and
- can be downloaded as PDFs from within the library community.

Our digital library collections are a great solution to beat the rising cost of textbooks. e-books can be loaded into their course management systems or onto student's e-book readers.

The **Business Expert Press** digital libraries are very affordable, with no obligation to buy in future years. For more information, please visit **www.businessexpertpress.com/librarians**. To set up a trial in the United States, please contact **Adam Chesler** at *adam.chesler@businessexpertpress .com* for all other regions, contact **Nicole Lee** at *nicole.lee@igroupnet.com*.

Lightning Source UK Ltd.
Milton Keynes UK
UKOW030734070213

205963UK00009B/148/P